MW01687074

Happy reading!
Marisol xx

Marisol Michaud

You're Too Chicken

Translated from French

By Marie-Ève Couët

MARISOL MICHAUD

3800 Carré Bernard
Boisbriand (Québec)
J7H 1L1, Canada

Email : info@marisolmichaud.com
Website : www.marisolmichaud.com

Translation : Marie-Ève Couet
Correction : Marie-Ève Couet et Arella Bryn
Graphic design : Catherine Parke
Covers : Julie Normandin et Renée Champagne
Photographer : Maryline Tremblay

Cataloguing in Publication of Bibliothèque et Archives nationales du Québec and Library and Archives Canada

Title : You're too game / Marisol Michaud.
Names : Michaud, Marisol, 1981- auteur.
Description: Includes bibliographical references and an index.
Identifiers : Canadiana 20190029250 | ISBN 9782981922939 (soft cover)
Subject headings : RVM : Change (Psychology) | RVM : Self-actualization | RVM : Neurolinguistic programming.
Classification: LCC BF637.C4 M53 2019 | CDD 158.1-dc23

To my daughters Abigaël, Mérédith
and Madison

BONUS

I prepared a little something for you that will allow you to experience this book even more intensely. It's hard to believe, I know!

Just check it out @
www.marisolmichaud.com/bonus-book

This book is written in the feminine form to facilitate its reading.

Nothing more to it.

Happy reading.

WARNING

1. All the anecdotes shared in this book have been revamped and the names have been changed to preserve client confidentiality.

2. You'll quickly get hooked to the story telling.

3. If you find yourself questioning something you read and think there might be a mistake, I can assure you that's not the case. All the wording has been carefully thought through to trigger reactions. Get used to it!

Exercise before reading

Answer the following questions with the first thing that comes to mind.

Who are you?

If you had a magic wand, what would you immediately change?

What are the challenges that prevent you from getting what you answered in the previous question?

Sexy Table of Contents

(Sounds silly but we brainstormed to find a sexy title to the table of contents but nothing good came up so we decided to call it just that).

INTRODUCTION

I've been wondering for weeks about how to begin this book in an effective and remarkable way. Remarkable because there is nothing ordinary about this book. Not even this introduction. In fact, I would call this section a warning. This book, as you've probably already noticed, is not like the others. I know that's what everyone says about their book, or at least I hope so, but this time it's actually true. You may not know me yet, but the pages of this book were written the only way I know how: all-in!

As with all artists, writers, singers, actresses, etc., vulnerability is necessary to be able to deliver a part of oneself and therefore, risk being judged. In this book, you will find the gist of my philosophy since NLP (Neuro-Linguistic Programming) came into my life. I'm sharing with you everything I have, everything I am, how I think and how I function, like I've never done before. With humility, as much as possible, because I know I'm fucking awesome. How can I ask people for vulnerability if I don't start with myself? If you want this book to bring you all that it's capable of, you're going to have to jump into it with that same vulnerability. In addition to experiencing an outpouring of realizations, anecdotes and truths, you will see all my colors, my sometimes sharp humor and my own realizations from the last few years.

I have been swimming in the self-help world for several years now and although it may seem beige at first glance, I decided to write more than 65,000 words about it! Self-help is not sexy per se but for someone who wants to feel in alignment, it can be! In this field, whether in training, conferences or books, what we find the most are inspiring stories and motivational speeches. And that's totally OK if you want to be motivated! After reading all my stories, my transformations and those of my clients, chances are, you will be. However, a few weeks after you've been exposed to this kind of motivational speech, once you're back to your daily routine and your thought patterns, what will you have left of those readings that instantly triggered a tornado in you? I'll tell you what. You are left with the same limiting beliefs and patterns that you've been carrying around for far too long and that continue to screw up your life and push you to self-sabotage. Ouch, right? The self-saboteur, who I named The Gremlin, is a character who seems cute, soft, gentle and sweet, but once fed, turns into a real monster! So, if you want to still be in the same place in a year, do like most people; implement some motivational tips and put them in place for two weeks, three if you really rock. Then, since it won't change anything in your life and you won't get out of your comfort zone, put your trusty old slippers back on and move on OR, if you REALLY want change, keep reading.

Here in this book, it's going to be different. In addition to becoming highly motivated, I will help you change your unconscious. I believe in spontaneous transformation and lasting behavioral change in humans, having experienced it myself and seen it in several thousand clients. And that' s exactly what I am offering you.

The question that remains is: Are you badass enough to go through everything I have to offer? If you don't want to work on your shit, or should I say your bullshit (I know we're classy queens but let's keep it real, ok?), if you don't understand what I'm talking about when I say "wanting to make your life better", if you don't have the real desire to clean up your life, to have ease and happiness in all spheres of your life and if you're not truly ready to live a life in alignment with who you really are – then don't read this book! And I'm saying this with all the love and kindness in the world, to save you from wasting your time.

It's not a bad thing that there are so many tools to motivate human beings. They really are necessary! It's also why coaches, all fields combined, exist. However, some coaching methods are designed to make you feel like you need intensive or extensive sessions to achieve results which creates a sense of dependency. The fact is that it's possible to get permanent results without spending fortunes or years in therapy.

Wouldn't you find it easier if you were to stay as motivated as the day you decided to take action? You know, the day you say to ourselves, "That's it! Starting today, I'm gonna work out every single day!" No, no! I'm not talking about myself here! It's the story of a girl my friend told me about.

But seriously, who's never said that? You and I know that the morning we make this resolution, we are fully committed to our decision. We mean it, we live it, nothing can stop us. And what happens after 24 hours, or a few weeks for some? The goal is still there, or at least some traces of it, but the motivation has completely gone out the window!

So, what is the percentage of people who actually achieve their goals? And how do they do it?

Humans need to be motivated, we all agree on that. Did you know that from birth, we have genetically created programs in our brain that prevent us from coming out of our comfort zone? Did you know that with optimal shifts in consciousness, you create new neural connections that will allow you to think and act differently in a split second? I am telling you that you CAN easily reach your goals. For real. Are you ready to accept this information? What do you choose to get you to your destination: an A1 car or a car that can break down at any time?

By reading these pages, you're readying yourself for a tune-up so that you can get to all your dream destinations without getting stuck because of faulty brakes, wipers or even worse – engine problems! How do we make sure that our car will accomplish the mission for which it was created? We do maintenance throughout the year. So how do you make sure you're at your best and that you're A1 all year round so that you can make all your wildest dreams come true and live your life in alignment with who you really are?

If you have doubts about what I'm promising you in this book, then test it out! There are no guarantees unless you take the necessary actions. If you agree to soften your beliefs, open your world map (I will discuss this in more details in the bonus chapter) and change your perceptions. If, as you read this, you feel a little pinch in your heart, a lump in your stomach and thoughts like: "*This can't be true. This kind of life is not possible. Not for me anyway*" starts flooding your mind, well just keep reading and you'll see.

And I, in return, promise to be honest and authentic. I won't embellish the panic attacks, the "bawling my eyes out in the fetal position" moments and all that regaining power over your life and taking responsibility for it involves. I also promise to introduce you, in the humblest way possible, to all the corners of reality through the process of personal growth. The not always zen side of what is required when it comes to dealing with your state of mind on a day-to-day basis.

I'm repeating myself, but it's important for me that you understand that you've just opened a Pandora's box! Working on yourself is an eternal journey towards becoming the best version of yourself, yes, but most of all towards uncovering who you really are and what belongs to you in all this hodge-podge of beliefs and thoughts! Are you still here?

When you start working on yourself, you may get discouraged and feel that you have moved backwards rather than forward. What's more, (seriously, I'm not encouraging you getting through this book), the further we go, the more we have to be malleable and question everything that defines us. This implies constant check-ups, just like on your car!

If you're still with me at the end of this book, I guarantee you will experience some changes, starting from the very first chapters. I'm not gonna sugar-coat it so get ready to be blown away! So again, if you're not ready, save yourself some quality time and give my book to your best friend because, as you will learn in a little bit, when you change, it changes everyone around you. In fact, you'll feel the benefits of your friend's changes second-handedly. Yes, I sometimes have a mischievous option hiding not too far behind the righteous first idea!

Obviously, as you've surely already noticed in your environment, there are different levels of consciousness, different stages in the process of working on yourself. Whether you are on your first book of mindset stir-up or your twentieth, you will get exactly what you need right now. Several of my clients have told me that if they'd known the level of transformation they would accomplish, they would have come to me sooner. But everything happens for a reason. The results we achieved together would not have been the same if they hadn't gone through what they went through first. On the other hand, maybe they would have. We'll never know for sure. The important thing is to keep the focus on you, and how you're feeling right now.

If you know a little bit about personal growth and coaching, you will see that I mainly use NLP tools, some of which I developed myself. I also include everything I have discovered in the last few years, which allows me to facilitate spontaneous transformations and lasting changes in humans. This includes EFT, Access Consciousness, hypnosis, meditation, impact therapy, Reiki, Brain Gym, several Tony Robbins training programs and so on!

The idea for me is that yes, I chose NLP to make a difference in people's lives, but I think that finding the approach that speaks to us and that we believe in is really the most important thing! Did you know that there's a medical study showing that 100 people who were diagnosed with terminal cancers of several types, were eventually considered in complete remission (a minimum 10 years without any symptoms). When questioned about what had helped them heal, they all had very different methods ranging from changing their eating habits, to more esoteric methods, to doing nothing. The only thing they had in common was a strong belief that what they had chosen to do would heal them. We always say that the power of the mind changes everything, but WTF! Our beliefs have the power to heal ourselves (or not) from a terminal cancer diagnosis... Anyways... I'll let you stew on that for a bit before we get back into it later.

Are we doing this now or what?

CHAPTER 1
My Pledge

Here's what will happen to you if you implement a few of the tools from the set I'm about to give you. Whenever you feel some resistance because of your values and beliefs, cut yourself some slack. Cutting yourself some slack means that you give yourself a break for a couple of minutes, you think about something else and you put up with a little discomfort in order to experience the magic:

— Feeling liberated from a ton of stuff that you've been hanging on to for far too long;

— No longer feeling guilty about everything;

— No longer being so demanding of yourself;

— Cutting yourself some slack;

— Getting everything you want out of life.

My last bullet could be considered “magical thinking”, I know, but that's where you're wrong. You're going to expand your world of beliefs, which by the way, defines who you are (or who you think you are). Plus, you will make a multitude of realizations that will modify your attitudes, your behaviors and above all, your perception of reality or what it has supposedly been.

Now that the warning about what awaits you has been given, I must inform you that it's already too late to back down. Everything you have just read since the beginning of the chapter has already been set in motion. Without you realizing it, new neural connections in your subconscious are forming that will already have an influence on the perception you had of your reality. *Really?* you say to yourself. *Yeah right!* Yes, it's as simple and as easy as that. It hasn't been too painful to work your shit up until now, right? Let's keep going...

Here are a few important things that I would like to share with you about myself and some of my beliefs so that you can push your transcendental, cosmic, planetary-like personal experience even further! Don't worry, everything will be alright.

First of all, an explanation of the phrase "we're in the right place". Sometimes, you experience a period of confusion after reading a sentence, feeling that you don't understand anything anymore, that you can't make sense of it, and that you have a "deer caught in the headlights" expression on your face (yes, the one where you freeze with your eyes wide open and don't understand what's happening to you or what just happened). This means that you're in the right place to change the way your brain works and, by the same token, change your life.

Then, know that another one of my goals is to tell you that just because you already have everything in your life, a job that you love, your dream life partner, perfect children, health, etc., doesn't mean that you don't have the right to want to be happy on top of that and to feel amazingly good on the inside. What you will quickly understand with me is that I firmly believe that life is infinite, that we are infinite beings and that we can have great abundance in all spheres of our lives. You read this right. Infinitely infinite! Beliefs such as: "I'd rather have less money and be healthy than be rich and super tired"; "You can't have it all-in life"; "You can't have your cake and eat it too"; "It's because he can't be satisfied with what he has and appreciate it"; etc. are not part of who I am. Who says you can't have it all?

I'm sure that when you read this last question and take the time to think about it, a name will pop into your head. You know very well where these expressions come from. Here, I'm generalizing as if everyone believes this, but from my experience, the majority of us have to make an update on this belief.

VIP Retreats

Let's take as an example one of my VIP retreats. The concept of my retreats always takes place at a fabulous location. We are completely lost, alone in the world in the woods or by a lake, in small groups of women for a 48-hour retreat like they've never experienced before. They may know me and know what I do and how I work, but during these VIPs, we dive into unsuspected hidden corners of their personalities and their life experiences. When I say it like that, I realize that it sounds like the participants either have no idea what they're getting into and are really naive, or they're really brave, or they're just completely crazy! So, we're lost in the woods, with only the sound of leaves rustling in the wind. Do you get the picture?

Among other things, participants must do an exercise that works on their ability to receive. I gotta say that no matter how beautiful your requests to the universe are and even if you put all the necessary actions into place, if you are unable to receive, you will only get the crumbs of what could be a tsunami of abundance. It may sound harsh but that's the way it is. I'm not talking about getting a slice of pizza because you helped a friend move, that's called making a service exchange. I'm talking about a way of receiving in which you don't even say thank you back, you just take it. Just taking. It's possible that this last sentence makes you look like a deer caught in the headlights. Not saying thank you in return for something; sacrilege! Good. If that' s the case, then it means that there is already something different going on inside of you.

So, the participants finish their exercise and one of them, a successful lawyer, shares with us that she wasn't able to do it because she feels guilty about receiving more than she already receives from life: "I like the way I look. I have a boyfriend who's good to me and healthy children. I really don't have any financial issues. I have a job that I love. So why should I get more out of life? I can't, it would be too much!" To which I of course asked, "And why not?"

If this woman is with me in this retreat, at this moment, it's because there's something that could be better or aspects of her that she would like to be free of. Right? Why, in addition to everything she already has, shouldn't she have the right to feel a sense of well-being on a daily basis? Why shouldn't she have the right to taste the joy of living constantly, on top of everything she already has? The fact that she studied law, that she's in a relationship, that she has children, justifies that she shouldn't want to feel good on the inside also? I mean, it would really take the cake if she were happy all the time, on top of having everything else! It would really be the cherry on top! Because of the abundance in all the other aspects of her life, it's fair that she struggles mentally and feels an intense lack of well-being? It just doesn't make sense to me! Are you starting to get the point about receiving?

If, while reading these last few words, you had thoughts like: *Oh my god, the girl's a lawyer, makes lots of dough, is in a relationship and has kids on top of it, what the hell is she complaining about?*

I can tell you that these thoughts are more about you than the lawyer or even the richest, healthiest girl in the world. These thoughts represent your current limitations. They represent what you might want, what you might aspire to and what you don't dare have, either by blocking your beliefs, through lack of confidence, through fear of being disappointed, through fear alone. If you think I'm exaggerating, you're not the only one. Countless times, I would even say 99% of the women I've been in contact with over the years, at some point thought like you. The advice I can give you right now is that in life, you want to move up, you want to work on being and giving the best version of yourself, not the other way around. So allow yourself to question everything you believe in as you read these lines. Give yourself this gift. I choose the word *gift* wisely because on the other side of our beliefs and judgments lie freedom and lightness. The second you allow yourself this gift in front of others, you also give it to yourself. I reassure you, it's not *all* of your beliefs that are limiting you right now, but let's live all-in and dangerously by putting everything in the blender of change, shall we?

Also, I've never heard anyone tell me: "I try to piss off as many people as I can, so I can really feel alive and fulfilled." I've never heard anyone say that, ever. Even from people who really *do* piss people off! Don't waste energy being jealous of the person next door, because that time and energy is gone forever. Stay focused on you, on your own progress. I'm sharing this cautionary note with you. Just like that. Just in case. But I know very well that you would never be jealous of another woman, of her success and her achievements, because that's not you at all; you're my reader, after all! You're already qualified as an exceptional human being!

There's a business network, created in Quebec by Christine Marcotte, called *Le Réseau des Mères en Affaires,* where mothers who've decided to become entrepreneurs can get together and talk about their businesses. Since I am a partner in this network, women who become members get a free consultation with me. When they make an appointment, sometimes it's not because they are experiencing a real problem or know about me but because my services are included in their membership. So, sometimes, on D-Day, when I ask them what I can do for them, they don't know. I ask them if there is something bothering them in their lives, a particular problem that I could help them solve and they tell me that everything is fine. They've heard that what I do is awesome, but they have no idea what I can do for them. Yeah right, you get in touch with a coach but you don't have anything you wanna work on to make your life better...

Your subconscious tells me that you didn't book this meeting just for fun and that there's a part of you that wants to receive more!

And there are also women who tell me that they are OK when in fact, they just settle for what they have. I know this because when I ask them THE question, it goes like this: "If you had a magic wand, what would you wish for?"

All of a sudden, a bunch of ideas pop into their heads like popcorn! It's as if eliminating all the boundaries and using magic allows them to ask for more. A moment ago, they had nothing to complain about.

So I am asking you, looking deep into your eyes: Are you really open? And most of all, are you ready to live a life of abundance in all aspects?

As for me, in short, for my whole life I followed the path already traced for me by society, the one that you *must* follow to find "success". The one that says you have to go to school and get a good job. You know that famous path that sells us the idea that we have to find a spouse, get married, have children and buy a house in order to live "happily ever after".

I took this path. I survived this path. I say *survived* because on that road, I met with depression. In fact, it had already been building its nest for several months before someone reflected to me that I was already right in the middle of it. Like Samantha in the movie *Sex and the City* when Carrie, Charlotte and Miranda make her realize that she is no longer in love with Smith. Sorry for the girly reference, but apart from my alternative side which I love, I have more than one string in my bow!

So one day, I showed up in a coach's office with my partner at the time, far from wanting to seek help for myself. We're in her office that morning because one of our daughters has been pulling her hair out for over a year. Not one hair left on her head. The coach starts the session by asking us THE question:

— How are you?

We are fine. For real! In the hustle and bustle of everyday life we're caught up in, we are fine. Two children under the age of two. Temper tantrums. Not getting a full night's sleep for over six months. Arguments over arguments about the most insignificant things. I'm doing fine. For real! And the coach adds:

— You two, the relationship, how's it going?

Insert cricket noise here... What relationship? We don't have time for that anymore. The truth is that we haven't taken any time off as a couple for quite some time now. The conclusion of this meeting: I've been suffering from severe depression since I don't know when. My partner is in a burnout state. It's not fine at all.

The reason I'm writing this book today is that after this first meeting in NLP, my daughter never pulled her hair out again. Not once. On my ready-made path, I did a master's degree in biochemistry. When I saw the impact of our first meeting on my daughter's behavior, I wanted to understand how it all worked. My scientific side took over.

After coming out of depression (a process that lasted only a few months, without medication, through weekly NLP consultations only), I completed the entire NLP training. In 2016, I resigned from my job as a college level chemistry teacher to become my own boss by creating my empire in NLP coaching. Since then, thousands of women have seen their lives completely transformed. My NLP program has been offered in the international French-speaking community and is in the process of being translated in English for more than 46 countries around the world. And even after all this, going from biochemist to entrepreneur, going through an unhappy marriage, learning to completely respect myself in my relationships, increasing my income by 25 times in eight months, I must confess that I still have a personal coach who allows me to push the boundaries of what is possible for me even further than what I believe in. Chills?

To think that all these changes were achieved only through the transformation of my beliefs. Knowing that no matter who we are, no matter where we come from, we all have the potential to change and create a life that exceeds our expectations is now what drives me every morning!

In order to begin this quest that you may not have even suspected when you bought this book, I suggest a first exercise: the wheel of life. By the way, if you've already completed the various exercises I'm going to share with you throughout this book, don't hesitate to do them again in a few months and in a few years. Because as of tomorrow, you will already be tomorrow's version of yourself and not today's version. You evolve, you grow, you move forward. So, allow yourself to update who you are right now and to give yourself the benefit of the doubt that you will surely continue to understand and gain new awareness and new ways of looking at things.

Exercise: The Wheel of Life

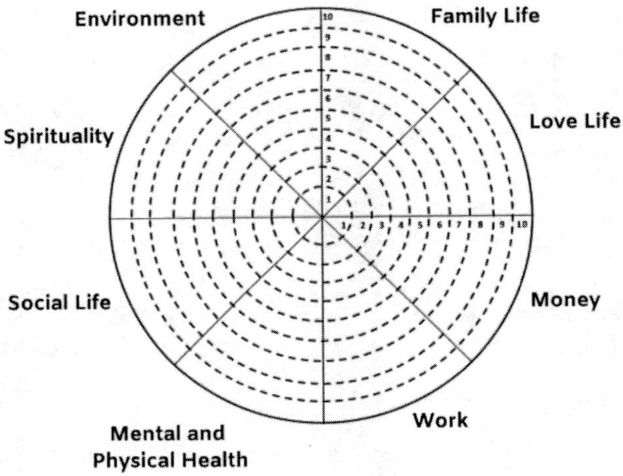

Draw a circle separated into eight equal parts and name each of the wedges with the following topics: environment, family life, love life, money, work, mental and physical health, social life and spirituality. If you are not familiar with this wheel, here is my definition of each section:

Environment: This theme represents the place where you live, the place you consider your home. Do you feel good? Safe? Do you feel that you can really be yourself there?

Family Life: Take into account the dynamics that you are currently experiencing with your children, your parents, your brothers and sisters, your mother-in-law, etc. How is it going? Are you currently experiencing conflicts with any of these people?

Love Life: This includes everything that happens in this area, whether you are in a relationship or not. Are you happy in your relationship? Are you happy being single if that' s the case or is this aspect of your life draining a lot of your energy?

Money: Ah, the infamous dough! If you knew how many limiting beliefs I've personally had to update and how many I hear from my clients about money on a daily basis, you'd flip! Are you experiencing financial stress right now? Are you working on becoming even more financially independent? Are you living in abundance on this level?

Work: How is your work life? Are you fulfilled by what you do every day? Do you feel like you belong? Do you feel comfortable in your work environment?

Health: It's important to consider the physical aspect as well as the mental aspect. I think that for your physical health, it' s pretty obvious. You know very well if you have been feeling in great shape lately or not. And as far as your mental health is concerned, how are you? Do you have strategies in place to make sure you're doing well in that area? Are you able to not let everything around you have power over your thoughts? Can you get rid of all the thoughts that are poisoning your existence?

Social life: Would you say right now that you are surrounded by extraordinary people who see you for who you really are and recognize your true value? Are you surrounded by people who *pull you up,* as they say? People who allow you to be yourself and inspire you to grow?

Spirituality: This is about observing, evaluating whether you feel connected to something bigger than yourself, to the universe, to whatever it is. How do you feel about being one human being among so many others on this planet? How do you deal with your soul? How is your search for meaning in this human reality going? If these last questions don't really resonate with you, no problem. Everything is OK, you'll see...

Then, take some time to evaluate each of the topics from 1 to 10, depending on how you are currently feeling about them (1 being really bad, 10 being really awesome). This exercise will allow you to take a step back and realize where the crux of the matter is in your life right now, in order to set the domino effect in motion. Your first change will trigger a series of changes without you having done anything else. This exercise will also allow you to get the big picture of what you're feeling right now to compare with how you feel at the end of this book and observe the evolution.

For example, say you rate 6-7/10 in most areas of your life but in your social life, you rate a 3/10. Even if you are under financial stress or your children are beyond disorganized right now, you should start making changes to your social life. As you'll see in greater detail below, everything is interconnected. This change will necessarily influence all other spheres of your life. Choose three actions that you're going to do right now to bring change to your lowest scoring category and see what happens.

CHAPTER 2

Santa Claus

You have to work hard to succeed in life. You have to work hard to deserve what you have. You have to go to school in order to get a good job. Starting your own business is tough so it's normal to have skinned knees for the first five years. Well, of course it's easy for him, his father was there before him.

How does it feel reading this? How about I add a little more?

Men don't cry. It's unbecoming for a girl to have strong character. Don't do that in front of people! Stop shouting, the neighbors will hear you!

All these beliefs are false. Everything you believe in, everything your world is built upon comes from your parents. And everything that your parents believe or believed in comes from their parents, so from your grandparents, who also learned from their parents and so on. These are just thoughts and beliefs that have been passed down from generation to generation without ever getting updated. What the fuck, huh?

I even read that being connected to our emotions is not part of our education in North America due to the early settlers who didn't have time to prioritize their emotions. When your life is at stake and your main concern is doing whatever you must to stay alive, taking time to introspect is not really a priority. But nowadays, our reality is quite different, right? Human interaction and communication are very much integrated into our daily lives and raising our awareness is also now part of where we're at in our evolution as humans.

Do you agree that an update in our beliefs is long overdue?

Like everything else, our beliefs are there for a reason. Their purpose is to take care of our doubts and define a reality that we can trust, build on and use to move forward in our lives. On top of that, for the most part, they were passed on to us when we were between 0 and 8 years old, when our conscious mind had not finished developing and couldn't do its job of filtering out what did and didn't fit with our personality. If our parents were able to make us believe that a fat man dressed in a red suit came through the chimney to bring us presents, can we agree that we believed *everything* we saw, heard and experienced during childhood? We bought into all those cheap beliefs and thought patterns as children and now they've become million-dollar beliefs that we're willing to defend as if our lives depend on it!

Let's take a random (#not) belief as an example. You believe that if your children sleep in the same bed with you, they're going to become dependent and you'll have to deal with all kinds of temper tantrums, turning them into spoiled brats who always get the last word. They won't understand that their job as children is to sleep in their own bed and that it's the adults who call the shots. Don't get me wrong, I believe in respect. I believe that it's important to show our children by example that there are many of us living together on this planet and that if everyone did as they pleased, it would be anarchy. But what if you want to comfort your child by sleeping in the same bed? If you, according to your values, consider this a part of the memories you want to create? Does it matter who's right between those who think that sleeping in the same bed as their children makes them dependent and demanding or those who prefer to follow their instincts that tell them the best thing for their children, at that time, is co-sleeping? What really matters is that YOU know what's important to you and that your actions make sense with the parent you want to be. That's it.

During one of my famous retreats (what can I say, I love working in country houses with fireplaces and hot tubs), one of my clients tells us that when she was little, she was already overweight. One day, walking down the street with her mother, she pointed out to a thin girl across the street and whispered to her:

"Look Mommy, she's so beautiful." And then her mother said, "Yes, but honey, at least you're smart." I don't know if you can see the kind of distortion this could have created in my client's mind when she was barely 10 years old. All her life she thought to herself that she might be fat, but at least she was smart. It even made her think that all the beautiful women who were successful in their businesses were only so because of their good looks and nothing else! Can you imagine how nearly impossible it was for her to lose weight? All the energy she put into it ended up in self-sabotage when she'd manage to lose a few pounds. She'd end up gaining back almost twice the weight she'd lost. Why is that? If she really lost weight, she thought she'd become stupid? Of course, all of this was in her subconscious. Amazing, isn't it? The point here is not to panic or think that everything you've ever believed in is all a bunch of lies. The goal is really to make you realize that some of your beliefs are probably ruining your life right now and I think it's time to put an end to that.

If you were game enough to take my book home with you and you're reading it right now: 1. You have shown courage. 2. I think you're definitely having a hard time with something in your life. And I would stake my life on the fact that it's precisely because you've tried to reproduce what you've been taught and you've truly tried everything you could to fit in with what you've been given in this generational transmission of beliefs. I'm telling you that there's a good chance your struggle comes from the fact that this legacy doesn't work for you. And that has nothing to do with whether your parents were good parents or not. Anyway, we're not here to judge but to take back power and ownership over our lives. Putting the blame on what's happening to us and what we've experienced on whoever or whatever is to give it too much power.

You've used the strategies you've learned your whole life, most of which come from your environment during childhood. You might want to, often subconsciously, reproduce their ways, honor them and be loyal; but it doesn't work. So much so that it makes you sick or close to it. You get exhausted, you look for happiness, you look for the meaning of everything you're going through and then niet, nada, nothing. So, the burning question right now is: are you ready to live this life that is yours, free of all chains and ties?

And when I say *free*, I mean truly free! Do you think that among your beliefs, there are helpful ones and others that are limiting?

What if I told you that they're practically all limiting?! Even the ones you call helpful. Okay, I know, I know, I just told you the opposite a little earlier; I didn't wanna scare you, but read all the way through first.

You're probably thinking: *Okay, but what's left if everything I believe in limits me in the end? How do I know if it's a good belief or not?* Beliefs are used to build the world and therefore, the reality in which we evolve. We believe in certain things that we think are true without a doubt, that we don't question, so we can move on and put our focus on something else. These beliefs help us for a while. But there comes a time when what you believed 20 years ago, without realizing it, no longer makes any sense to who you are and who you strive to become. It confronts you each day with a reality that you're trying so hard to get rid of. That's why it's important, from time to time, to update all your thoughts! Never forget that our thoughts create our reality.

For example, when I was with the father of my children, I believed that everything had to be done equally in a relationship. You know the "I'll do this in exchange for that" deal, which quickly turns into "I'll do this if you do that". I was constantly disappointed because, of course, I always felt like I was doing more than he was. Regardless of whether that was true or not, there's no way to be objective when you are completely emotionally involved in a situation. The only thing that was true for sure was, that was how I felt. My attention was completely directed, to the point of distortion, on keeping track of who did more than the other. You know, the most pernicious thing about beliefs is that they define your reality so much that your brain will go as far as to look for what confirms them.

Here's another example: you once had a spouse who cheated on you and so you bought the belief that all men cheat on their wives. Again, no judgments about cheating. It's just an interesting point of view as to whether or not such a thing is right or wrong. So, you embark on a new relationship and start checking your boyfriend's texts and his comings and goings. You don't want to get hurt and, once again, be played the fool. You analyze his every move, you test him on what he says, etc. At some point, you discover a message in which he's sending kisses to a friend. It'll be more of a relief to find that message than to not find anything at all. Finally, you'll be able to confirm your belief and say, "I knew it! I was right to be suspicious and not trust him!" It's more comforting to confirm a belief that screws up your life than it is to realize you were wrong. Can you imagine what this means? I don't know if you're like me but even though I've known for quite some time now that the human brain works like this, even though I've made several updates, I can't help but watch the movie of my life play out in my head and notice how all my current beliefs have an influence on what I'm experiencing. You probably realize by reading these lines that if you are walking around right now with such baggage, thinking that all men are liars, you are unlikely to ever have a fulfilling relationship. Protecting yourself because you've been hurt also means protecting yourself from the beautiful things that could happen to you. We' re protecting ourselves from *everything* when we do that! Furthermore, living this way is living like a shadow in your own life.

Let's come back to my example. I was in a relationship with my husband and I was brooding over everything I was going through because of this awesome belief that everything between two spouses had to be done equally. Until the day I transformed that belief. It became: "Just because it's not equal, doesn't mean it's not fair." Specifically, just because I make dinner and take care of the kids every day and you mow the lawn once a week, that doesn't mean it's not fair. That's not the way it works. Not everything is a scoring competition. We will analyze this fact in more detail later. Thanks to this change in perception, I was finally able to recognize all that my spouse was doing for our family, in addition to lowering my expectations; and magically, he started to become more involved.

Another one of those beliefs that sneaks into our heads and, without us realizing, takes up the entire space, is the classic limitation of our competencies. Someone once told us that we were not good at math or English or we experienced failure. This isolated event then defined what we thought of ourselves and subsequently influenced all of our perceptions and the opportunities that we had. It can be as simple as a girl never wearing yellow or gray because she was always told it didn't go with her hair color.

Beliefs are thoughts that we constantly repeat to ourselves and that come to define our daily life AND our future. They take up so much space that of the 60,000 beliefs we have on average each day, 98% of them are the same as the day and the week before.

Can you imagine that? Even the ones that have allowed you to survive a particular event at a point in time are eventually due for an update. Let's take someone who experienced rejection when they were young. She may have developed the ability to become a chameleon. No matter what the situation, she adapts herself in order to be appreciated. And you better believe it works like a hot damn!

All of this is based on experiences she had when she was younger that made her buy into the belief that if she were herself, she wouldn't be loved. Becoming a chameleon is a very clever strategy that allowed her to survive at one point in her life; but is it still helpful to her now? Yes, being a chameleon is now a part of who she is. It's also *her* in a way, but is she able to be herself completely? Do you know what it's like to be yourself without wondering and worrying about what others will think?

Besides, beliefs are little buggers that hang out together, like in a hive! When you think you've got the queen, you dig a little deeper and you realize that it was just a worker bee and that the true belief to work on is much more deeply rooted.

This is why I'm suggesting an exercise to empty your beliefs and find the Mother Belief of each of your systems. How do we do this? Think of something you believe in very strongly, so much so that it would be almost impossible for me to change your mind, even with ironclad arguments. Then say to yourself, "I believe... because..." and you continue like so until you find the source of that belief. The goal here is not to find the cause of your beliefs but rather the belief that created the sequence of other beliefs, kind of like reaching the middle of a Russian Doll. For example, you believe that the harder you work, the more you deserve what you have. So it would go: "I believe we have to work really hard to get what we want in life because otherwise it means we're lazy. I believe we're lazy if we don't keep ourselves super busy to the point of exhaustion." etc. Do you see how interesting and pernicious that is? If you think you're lazy unless you're overworked, according to your definition, how can you ever take it easy without judging yourself and without it influencing our self-worth?

Holding this belief means that having an "easy" life where nothing is complicated and you have practically everything you want without making much of an effort is *not OK*. Tasting success and abundance is *supposed* to be hard. I'm *supposed* to be tired if I've been working every day for two weeks. After that, I'll be allowed to "spoil" myself, rest and do nothing. That's how I realized the only valid reason in life I had for doing nothing was being mega-tired (btw, is there such a thing as "doing nothing"? What do you do when you do nothing? You watch TV, you clean the house, you read, you meditate, you listen to music, you take a nap and you rest... Anyway... enough said...). And in my case, being tired to the point of doing nothing takes a lot!

So, I made two highly liberating realizations about these beliefs. For one, I had to feel very tired before I could just chill out and watch Netflix. If I was feeling the slightest bit energetic, I had to do something for my business, my girls, my apartment, and so on. Who's on Netflix when their house is a mess? You can' t do that! You don't deserve to just chill! Second, I realized that I just don't get that tired from working all the time and doing all kinds of things. But in order to correspond to what society dictates and with what I know, I had to be tired after working and doing activities for a certain amount of time. I mean, I get tired sometimes! But I really have a lot of energy and a great ability to optimize and be disciplined. In fact, I'm able to accomplish a lot before I feel an ounce of fatigue. But I had this belief that if I did nothing while I was feeling fine or just a little tired, it would automatically make me a lazy procrastinator. Well, from that point on, I decided to put Netflix days in the middle of my weekday schedule. The result? I now also do what needs to be done on Netflix days and I stopped feeling tired because I was supposed to be tired according to standards other than my own. I'm an achiever and I own that! Obviously, behind that was the fear of looking like a show-off, being able to do a whole lot while most people can't.

The important thing is to be yourself and to change the world with that; that's what I believe now. As Dain Heer, co-creator of the Access Consciousness approach, would say: "Getting back to standards because that's supposed to be the right thing to do or because that's what most people experience is also a way of not honoring yourself."

Take the time to list 10 beliefs and go back to their source. Many may come from the same source, and all the better! There will be less work for you! In fact, just being aware of it already makes all the difference, you'll see...

Exercise: List of the Ten Beliefs That Are Currently Ruining My Life

Take the "because" part of your belief, the one that pops in your head right away, and go in deeper to the next belief until you find the core belief which is the starting point of that system. Don't worry if you don't find it right away, you can come back to this as things sometimes pop up progressively. Eventually, you'll also realize that everything is connected. More details on that in chapter 20.

Example:

I believe W because X.

I believe X because Y.

I believe Y because Z.

1. I believe... because

2. I believe

3. I believe

4. I believe

5. I believe

6. I believe

7. I believe

8. I believe

9. I believe

10. I believe

BONUS CHAPTER

NLP and World Maps

Very quickly, I will summarize NLP (Neuro-Linguistic Programming) in case you've never heard of it. A tool for communication and brief therapy, the NLP approach helps us develop successful behaviors by teaching us to mobilize our resources and use our senses.

Richard Bandler defines NLP as: "An education of the brain, a sort of instruction manual." The French journalist, author and lecturer Florence Servan-Schreiber says that NLP is: "A set of communication and self-transformation techniques that focuses on our reactions rather than on the origins of our behaviors. It favors the how rather than the why and offers observation tools to improve the perception of oneself and others. NLP also allows you to set goals and achieve them. It's a toolbox, where the key is the language and the use that each of us makes of our five senses and our bodies. Its goal: allowing us to program and replicate our own models of success."

Increasingly recognized throughout the world in a multitude of fields by its accessibility, NLP is one of the most advanced and effective methods currently available to address the challenges of communication between human beings.

Since we're all born with the same neural structure, our ability to do what we want depends essentially on how we manage our nervous system. Take, for example, Olympic champions and their ability to get up every morning and push themselves in their sport in such an exceptional way. This can be achieved by learning how to manage our nervous system! Crazy, right?

Thus, NLP is about learning and understanding our thought patterns (all of which come from somewhere, by the way!) and communicating more effectively with others and with ourselves.

The word "programming" refers to the way we code and store information in our brains. Our personal programming represents the thought patterns (internal strategies and processes) we use for everything:

- Making choices;
- Making decisions;
- Managing life's daily challenges;
- Etc.

Thanks to NLP, we can now re-encode these thought processes and reorganize them to achieve the desired results.

Next, the word "neuro", for the neurological system. NLP suggests that the experiences we have depend on the internal representation of a situation through our five senses and that information is then transformed into thought processes, both consciously and unconsciously. Thus, these processes activate neurons that influence your physiology, emotions and behaviors. This is confirmed by the fact that we're not only our genetics! Actually, we are who we are because of the genes we have *activated,* which occurs about 30% from our genetics and 70% from our environment. This means that if the same two half-cells that make up your being were transported to another environment, you would not have become who you are today. Pretty incredible, isn't it?

A newborn comes into the world with more than 100 billion neurons that will mature, connect with each other and then develop a specialization. The experiences we had as babies, from our senses in the first months of life, directly shaped the architecture of our brains. Remember, I told you that all of our behaviors and thought patterns came from somewhere.

So, because of the phenomenal number of synaptic connections between two neurons that occurred as we experienced life after our birth, our brain "matured", in the sense that some neurons were activated and others were not. This created a balance between what made us, as a brand new human being, and the physical and social environment we lived in.

I don't know if after reading these last paragraphs you got as many chills as I have writing this. But the existence and the power of NLP at this very moment allows me to believe in the real changes in human beings, in their fast and durable change and also fills me with hope that no matter where we come from, we can be who we want to be.

One of the presuppositions of NLP is that the map is not the territory. Basically this means that what you *perceive* of your reality (your map) is not reality itself (the territory) because your map is created according to your senses, your beliefs, your values, etc. It is therefore extremely influenced when it's being created. And it's the same for all human beings. We all have these filters that make our perception of reality biased. Using expressions like "Open your world map" or "That's not part of my map" helps you make sure you're keeping an open mind and you're not limiting yourself to your own map. A person who opens up his or her world map, who allows themselves to think that there's something other than what they've known for years, opens themselves up to an infinite number of possibilities. And just because you agree to open your perceptions, that doesn't necessarily mean you'll adhere to those of others. You're only going to open yourself up to what exists. The more you are aware of this, the more you'll see all your relationships improve and an increase in the power you have over your life.

CHAPTER 3

WOWZAPALOOZA

Before I continue with the presentation of concepts, I would like to get something straight. You won't be able to make the changes you want if you don't start by becoming the main character of your own life! I know it sounds cliché and it's probably nothing new to you. There are going to be a few little rules to follow and most likely some personality grooming. In order to help you with this, I am presenting you with one of my tools, which I call the "Wellness Scale". It's simple: imagine a color scale like the one you get for free at home renovation centers that you use to choose the color of paint on your walls. Also imagine that there are six levels on the scale. Now, without thinking about it, without saying to yourself, "What kinda question is that?", I would like you to answer the following. Come on! Let's go all-in!

If you were a color, which one would you be?

There are no right or wrong answers, and that goes for all the questions and exercises you will find in this book. Obviously, your answer does not need to be intellectualized. So, let's say you're pink; your wellness scale will start at the bottom in a very, very pale shade of pink which represents a "yucky" state where you're not doing well at all. And it will end at the top in a WOWZAPALOOZA shade of pink that you love.

The meaning of WOWZAPALOOZA, in case you didn't know, is quite simple. WOWZAPALOOZA is the hottest and most intense feeling of well-being you've ever experienced in your whole entire life. It's personal to each and every person, but there's a minimum feeling required to qualify for WOWZAPALOOZA. I don't hesitate to call it out to my clients in coaching. If their feelings are not WOWZAPALOOZA enough for my taste, they must find something else! To give you a good idea of what a WOWZAPALOOZA feeling is, remember a day when the weather was nice, when your mother-in-law was in a good mood, when your boyfriend made love to you like a god, when you went out to eat in your favorite restaurant, when you won the lottery and when the stars were all aligned! Having a WOWZAPALOOZA moment fills you up with an intrinsic happiness that makes you say to yourself: "Dear God, I'm so happy to be alive!"

I'm aware that I may be describing an extraordinary feeling that you've never experienced before. But know that one of my goals with these lines is to allow you to free yourself enough of everything you're holding on to so that you can also achieve this feeling of well-being. And not just randomly, but gaining the ability to create it over and over again.

That's why the idea is to place yourself, based on your current state, on your own scale of well-being. Take the time to realize how you're doing and understand that your current priority is to get to the top of your scale if you're not there yet. As I mentioned earlier, *you* are the priority in your own life. If you don't choose yourself first, who will? Before you resolve any conflicts with your family or your boyfriend, your child's behavior, your financial troubles or anything else, the first thing you need to do is take better care of yourself. On 3 together, let's become more selfish than ever before! 3, let's GO! Let's do what we love, let's set our limits (which involves saying *no* to people, by the way), let's make requests, let's allow ourselves to receive and also choose ourselves in everything we do. Let's put ourselves first. Now that's a small challenge you can take on right now, right?

One day, I decided to start using this color scale metaphor because every single client that came into my office, without exception, had low self-esteem and didn't make themselves a priority in their own lives. When you take the time to place yourself on your own WOWZAPALOOZA scale and realize that you have become a dull, faded version of yourself, it hits hard. And when you realize that you have no idea how you got there without recognizing that it was happening and you don't know how to make it out on your own, the shock is even greater.

For example, a client who comes to see me because she's annoyed that her husband isn't more involved with the household chores (100% fake example #yeahright). No matter how much I make her talk about herself, if I don't take the time to make her realize that she's a priority and that she needs to start putting herself forward again, working on her relationship will be useless. Working on your relationship when you're in the yucky part of your wellness scale produces the kind of results you can imagine. Furthermore, as we will later see, if the client realizes that she can get better and she takes responsibility for what she's going through, this will inevitably influence her partner's attitude and behavior. Once her own process begins and her system starts shifting, the right time to work on her relationship will come. If the need is still there.

The same goes for all the clients who have come to see me for behavioral problems or other issues with their children. Ninety-nine percent of the time, I don't ever meet with the children. Why is that? Because when the mother regains power over her life and starts to implement certain things in order to make herself a priority and care for herself, it enables the children's behavior to change. When the parents are doing OK, the children are doing OK.

As you can see, while it is important to learn to communicate well and to optimize our interpersonal relationships, learning about ourselves is even more important. When I say this, I don't mean knowing about what we like, the kinds of activities we wanna do, how to take care of ourselves and how to fulfill our needs – which is already a lot, according to my clients. For me, learning about ourselves means knowing why we react the way we do and knowing ahead of time how we're going to react to a particular situation. Most people experience all kinds of emotions and don't understand themselves. They don't understand why they suddenly feel disappointed, angry, sad, or even happy. Another fake example: a radio host has just told a very trivial anecdote. The listener suddenly starts feeling very uncomfortable, for no apparent reason. This person's reaction comes from an accumulation of not setting their limits with their spouse on a particular subject six months prior. At that very moment, she explodes! If she doesn't know herself well enough, she won't be able to connect the silly anecdote with her emotional build-up and she will be overwhelmed by the unpleasant emotion that was just triggered. And potentially for a very long time.

To better understand our emotions, we must necessarily dive into our vulnerability, take a step back and really observe what's going on inside us. We might need to trace our thoughts back to exactly what was happening when we started feeling uneasy, angry or anxious. Thanks to the scale, you'll better comprehend where you are and what's really at play. If you feel as though all the stars are aligned and you're overall doing great, then you are at the top, in the WOWZAPALOOZA zone. On the contrary, if you don't feel so good, you're going down the scale until you eventually reach the bottom level, the yucky zone. Someone going through depression is not even operating in their color scale anymore. They've completely forgotten who they are, they are only a shadow of themselves, in a grey shaded zone. If that's the state you're in and it's been going on for a while now, please get help and don't stay alone in this. If it's been a few months and you continue to endure because you think it's gonna go away, please, seek out counseling. When you're depressed, you're running on fumes. It's like we all have a full tank of gas to get through the day. Let's say we need 10 ounces for the morning routine, 5 for the laundry, 40 for our work day, etc. Someone who's depressed has about 10 ounces for the whole day and they need 25 just to get up in the morning, shower and get ready. Sometimes, just the thought of getting out of bed makes them feel burnt out. Remaining in this situation by yourself without any help may add to the number of years it takes to recover. With proper support, the process can take anywhere from a few weeks to a few months. So choose yourself now if that's the case.

When you're at the lowest level of your color scale, you're OK enough to put some actions in place and create change in your life. Take the time to observe where you're at right now. It's not uncommon, even during a conference, for people to land more towards the bottom of the scale. As you know, putting yourself first and choosing yourself in all spheres of your life is not what we've been taught as children and that is why people often find themselves at the bottom and seek counseling.

In short, the first step is to take care of yourself in order to regain your energy. People who seek counseling for their partner or their children should regain their own strength first before doing anything major because it's not when we're doing really badly and we're overwhelmed by emotions that we make the best decisions! Right?

So, this color not only represents you but also your values, beliefs, experiences and what you arrive with when you interact with other people. For example, if you're blue, people are going to come up to you and say, "Wow, what a fun kind of blue! It's different from my red and from every other color I've ever been in contact with!" This tool helps you see all the things you bring to others, recognize yourself and become aware of where you come from and what you pass down to your children. As a result, if a blue person meets a red person and they have kids, well then, the kids are bound to be purple.

Yes indeed! We never fall far from the tree. We are who we are due to 30% genes and 70% our environment, which is what our parents are and what they gave us when we were kids. These little purples are going to take what they want from each of their parents (even if one parent is absent or has detrimental behaviors) and build their own color. A little side note for separated women: sometimes it's your ex-spouse's color that necessarily imprints on your child who then starts to really get under your skin when coming back from dad's apartment.

I once had a client who realized that what she found difficult was having to conform to the purple passed down by her parents while deep inside, she felt she was turquoise... This realization enlightened her on a whole area of her childhood, relieved her and took away all the pressure she put herself under to be loyal (more towards her parents than towards herself) and to conform. I know it sounds crazy, but human beings need meaning. Once you make sense of all the issues and the shit you've been through, then comes liberation and a great feeling of lightness.

Your homework for this chapter (yes, I give homework, I have every right to do so as this is my book and I'm a former teacher): you will have to list all the activities (minimum 20) that you like and that make you feel good. Some activities may take five minutes while others can take an entire weekend. These might include drinking tea, reading a book, going for a walk, taking a bath, etc. You'll see that after four or five, you already start to run out of ideas. And why is that? The majority of us haven't been taught to take time to feel and observe what our needs are and how to fulfill them. We've been on autopilot for so long that the last time we really knew and expressed what we wanted was when we were seven years old and only had ourselves to think about! It could also be that since becoming a mother, we've changed and we don't know what we really like anymore. Sometimes I have clients who work very hard for their business. They have the wonderful belief that you have to work hard to be successful and deserve it. And when they get rid of that lovely mantra and finally have time for themselves, they don't know what to do with it. Do they plan a happy hour? Should they go to the spa? Are they going to sit down to read? This so rarely happens! They want to make the most of this blessed moment and rock their me-time so badly that they end up disappointed. So, take the time to identify your color, take the time to observe where you are on the WOWZAPALOOZA scale and list a minimum of twenty activities that really cater to your needs. Not you ten years ago, you today. And do it without thinking about your budget, the amount of time you'd need, etc. Endless possibilities!

Exercise: List of Activities

Name twenty activities that make you feel like you're taking care of yourself and afterwards, you're completely re-energized, Zen and fulfilled.

1.

2.

3.

4.

5.

6.

7.

8.

9.

10.

11.

12.

13.

14.

15.

16.

17.

18.

19.

20.

CHAPTER 4

World Domination

Now I think it's the right time for me to tell you about a major observation I've made from my practice that many people don't know about. When remembering your childhood, more precisely your parents struggling with money or on the contrary, living in abundance, I'm willing to bet that at some point in your life, at school, at work, at home or by an adult who was an authority figure, this statement was passed on to you: "Sweetie, you have to work hard to get what you want in life." At that very moment, without realizing it, you concluded in your "unmatured" brain (FYI, the brain is fully mature around the age of 25, for most of us) that in life, not only do you have to work hard to get what you want, but if you don't, you are either lazy or a pro at procrastinating. In short, success is unlikely to be a part of your life.

Side note: I used the word "unmatured" on purpose rather than immature because you see, if I had said "in your immature brain", you might have thought I meant you were rather dumb. Dumb in reference to a young age when I'm really referring to a completely biological phenomenon. But the meaning we give to words is far from coincidental and says a lot about someone. I could easily draw your main thought patterns out just by listening to you talk for a bit. So, you could do just the same with the thousands of words I'm sharing with you in this book.

As we saw in chapter two, most of what we think and believe comes from our childhood. Nothing new so far. But what most of us have forgotten is that we can make the choice to do things differently. Okay, now you're gonna tell me, "I really don't do what my parents did, I've even spent my life trying to be different from them." And that's where you're wrong. I'm sorry to inform you in this way, without foreplay, but if you're reading these pages, it's because you want some change in your life. Or you love me deeply and you follow everything I do, that's also possible... Anyway, I bet you're looking for answers.

The fact remains that the reality you're living in right now, in all aspects, is the result of the actions and choices you've made so far. So, if you are not completely OK with your life right now, it means you've made certain choices that weren't completely aligned with who you are. I am telling you that you're already living your dream life! I hope your life is good right now... If not, don't worry, I won't leave you like this. I'm telling you all of this because you think you're doing something different from your lineage but in reality, if you're working hard to get there, if you're struggling, finding happiness in only a few areas, this means that you're still trying to be content with what you've been taught about what life *should* be. You're trying to fit into, according to your personality, what you were handed down. Fitting into all these unwritten rules that dictate what you wanna be and what you must do in this life, a decision which, may I remind you, is supposedly yours.

Please understand. All these people who explained life to you in their own way did it because they cared about you, because they didn't know how else to do it, because they too had a bad or a wonderful childhood, because they remained children even as adults and couldn't handle themselves. They did what they could with you, with what they'd been given. No matter the kind of childhood you had, and I mean NO MATTER, there are really no exceptions. I'm truly sorry if you had to go through some awful and unbearable experiences (although, I'm a little reassured that you knew what to do to arrive here, right now, reading this book), but all of these people did the best they could with who they were. Yeah, that's the cold harsh truth. And if you're feeling resentful reading this, then keep reading because there's another level of liberation ahead of you.

So, unless you've spent the last few years in coaching (sorry but for me, therapy doesn't really apply for that kind of instant major transformation), you're not going against your parents right now. Humans are what they are and they create a world for themselves according to what they know, what will be reassuring to them. This is what I call the uncomfortable comfort zone. And that's why you've been having such a hard time getting here. You've been trying to change yourself to fit into this explained reality instead of remaining yourself and creating the reality that fits you. Do you fully understand what I've just said? I'm going to say it again because when we hear things that make sense to us but aren't ready to hear it, our brain deliberately chooses not to understand. Instead of trying to change yourself in order to live happily in the reality that was created for you, be yourself and create your own reality.

"When a flower doesn't bloom, you fix the environment in which it grows, not the flower."

- Alexander Den Heijer

If the shit you just read is messing you up, if you think it can't be done, that it's not happening, that it sounds great but it won't do it for you, that you've already tried and it hasn't worked, that it's too good to be true. In short, if you have any thoughts other than "Yes, let's do this", know that you're just protecting yourself in order to stay in your uncomfortable comfort zone, in which you are as secure as you are unhappy.

What you don't know yet is that you are internally built for world domination, no less! You have an infinite power over your life that you're probably using only 0.00001% right now. It may sound daunting when you put it that way but for me, it's great news because it means that everything has yet to happen! We have the power to change everything we want in our lives. It's just that, one, we weren't taught how to do it (people can't teach you what they don't know) and two, it's all about being, not doing.

To better explain what this means in plain English, here's an example from a client. Sabrina is in her thirties, married with three daughters. Nothing alarming so far. She's at the head of her own business and of her family and she works really HARD to give herself and everyone she loves an incredible life, just like she's always dreamed of. One day, she comes to me because she has this impostor syndrome kicking her ass every time she's on the verge of achieving her goals. I'm telling you, this woman is just like all of us! After a few meetings, I dare (the word *dare* here is highly appropriate because it takes a shitload of love and kindness to support what I'm about to tell her) to share an observation with her about one of her daughters. What you need to know and what I haven't told you yet, is that Sabrina has a four-year-old daughter with a genetic syndrome, along with two three-year-old twins. You know, some people enjoy a full plate! Her four-year-old daughter has a global developmental disability and no one knows what she will or won't be able to do yet but what we do know now is that she's not sleeping through the night and she's not potty-trained.

So, with all this information in mind, I dare say to my client: "What if you believed that your daughter was capable of anything? And how about if you took the chance to give her infinite possibilities? What if, by giving her a chance, by not placing limitations on her right off the bat, your daughter could accomplish everything she wants, based on who she is?"

My client didn't take pleasure in putting limitations on her daughter. She was doing it because of what she'd been told, seen and read about other children diagnosed with the same syndrome. And, most importantly, she was doing it to protect both herself and her daughter from disappointment when she realized that her daughter had reached a plateau in terms of her abilities. You know, giving yourself hope that anything is possible and trying everything to finally come to the conclusion that it won't work. OUCH.

On that day, what I offered my client was the opening to a world of possibilities, but with no expectations. In life, we're not just *one thing*. We're not just mothers, women, sporty, nerds, and so on. There's an immeasurable number of things we can be and choose to be. Blocking ourselves from a multitude of options, without even knowing that they exist to begin with, is to deprive ourselves of our full potential in order to fit in with what has been dictated to us. Since that day, because my client agreed to let her guard down, to trust herself and her daughter, little Camille got a few full night's sleep and is now fully potty-trained (number one *and* number two). Can you imagine? And all this happened effortlessly, in two weeks! These results were achieved much more easily than my client had envisioned. What's more, I'm adding a little something to this anecdote because since then, she always sleeps through the night too! I have tons of stories like this one that I could share with you. But the story that interests me the most now is yours, which is about to be transformed.

To sum it up: if a client comes in for a consultation because of impostor syndrome and in addition to building her self-esteem and confidence, she sees her daughter being influenced by the changes she's experiencing, can you imagine how much the sky IS NOT the limit? Isn't it amazing? You can create this kind of change in all the areas we listed in the first chapter and do anything you want with it.

If you're here right now, as I mentioned before, there's a reason for that. And whatever that reason is, it has led you here. So while you're at it, why don't you take the bull by the horns and make the things in your life that you've always wanted to happen, happen? Having a love life that's tailor-made for you, having financial abundance, having people around you who appreciate you just the way you are, being healthy, being successful in your professional life, having everything you really want and much more! And all this depends on just one thing: You. And if you're starting to think that I'm living in a Care Bear world, well good!

Because it means that many of your beliefs and values have been shaken up and something can be done. Everything I put on paper, I've been through it and I've seen it happen in the lives of several thousand women. It's time for you to roll up your sleeves and take your rightful place in this life of yours. Even if it means swallowing your pride and admitting that you haven't made the best choices for yourself in the past. But hey, you did the best you could with who you were back then and that's perfectly fine. All of these events have allowed you to be here today, at the dawn of dominating your own life (and the world!), and that's what's most important here.

Are you one of those girls whose mindset is influenced by the weather? When there's a beautiful blue sky and the sun is shining, you feel happy, in a good mood and you even think to yourself that nothing bad can happen to you. When it's greyish, cloudy and rainy, you feel like curling up into a ball somewhere (#truestory, many of us are affected by the weather). So, if that's your case, it's about time you dive in deep to see what you're really made of and put some strategies in place. Strategies that will allow you to regain control over this famous mindset of yours so that it's no longer influenced by the weather. You're planning an outdoor activity next weekend and the forecast says it'll rain three days before the event. You decide to cancel and it's sunny after all. How many times has this happened to us? Sometimes, in the morning, they say it's going to rain and then it doesn't. Or the other way around, the day that was supposed to be beautifully sunny gets darker and it starts raining cats and dogs. All this weather blabber is just to say that we can have predictions, yes, but they're far from infallible. So if your mood depends on factors such as the weather, then it depends on something that's entirely random. It's not a big deal if you're influenced by the weather but get to know yourself, recognize it and put strategies in place to enter the mindset you want, when you want.

#worlddomination

That's what it means to regain full control over your life, babe! Don't be a #weathergirl.

CHAPTER 5

#workonyourshit

How did I come to dedicate an entire chapter to "working on your shit"? It's quite simple. I told you from the very beginning that I would be honest with you; you just have to believe in beautiful things and believe that you're entitled to them, for magic to happen in your life. There is, however, a necessary path to take first, also famously called "the process", in order to get to the other side of the fog. What fog am I referring to? From the very beginning of your life, you've been heading down your railroad tracks. The idea is to understand that you've never been on the wrong tracks and so it doesn't matter what you've been through or what you're going through right now. Really, it means that you've been through exactly what you were supposed to go through.

Sometimes, you simply experience small foggy passages on your journey. But the universe, fulfilling your requests, has offered you what you have in your life now. Yes, I said the word *universe*; I'm quietly placing my pawns. As you will see later, this is what I call "planting it". So, as you now know, you're currently living the life you've chosen.

To get a different result, you'll have to make different choices. And to make different choices, you'll have to transform your beliefs (limiting AND helpful), your perceptions, well, basically everything that defines you right now. You need to update your data and to be able to do that, you have to stop sticking your head in the sand, thinking that everything is fine and will just turn out OK without having to change anything. You'll have to make new realizations. It sounds simple but believe me, raising your consciousness to the point of making a "deer in the headlights" expression is a lot harder than just taking action. Making new realizations and questioning everything we've based our lives on can feel overwhelming at times.

Working on your shit is a cousin to the expression "getting your shit together", which means getting your life in order, moving directly towards your goal without goofing around. Whereas #workyourshit is about not hesitating to step into your vulnerability. It's about working on what needs to be worked on in spite of discomfort and fear.

What do I mean by *vulnerability*? It's that part of ourselves we're afraid to access, where we think we're going to discover things that will disappoint us and make us suffer. I won't lie, sometimes it hurts like hell. Sometimes we bawl our eyes out and sometimes not. I believe that working on one's vulnerability can also be done in a simple, fluid and non-painful way. But each time, I promise you almost instant relief. I say *almost* because sometimes, we know we got it. We know that this new way of thinking is right for us but we may need a little bit more time to assimilate things and come to terms with what we're leaving behind. Also, everyone has their own pace for transformation, their own process. It can also be contextual. For example, just because someone makes peace with their impostor syndrome in a single session, doesn't mean that it'll be the same for all of my clients. And even for that particular client, it may take a different turn when the time comes to transform her perception of her parents' abandonment.

I myself, who's guided people through incredible transformations on several issues at the same time in a single session, may need several sessions with my own coach. At times, it's been very frustrating! Why is it that in one meeting, I could help with a client's sense of financial insecurity, causing her to then experience incredible financial abundance, while I was still struggling with the same issue? I already knew that we each have our own unique process. That's when my coach and I realized that I operate in chains of cause and effect and that all of these chains are tightly intertwined, resulting in tremendously intense releases. It's also possible that they're a little more complex to undo. Each person is unique. Don't spend energy passing judgment on how you function, how you understand things and how long it takes you to achieve results. Don't be like me! Once again, the most important thing is getting to know yourself, respecting as much as possible the discoveries you'll make in this quest and, above all, allowing the extraordinary person you are to be valued. With time, we get used to navigating in this famous vulnerability zone or we simply become a bit sadomasochistic because we want more and more of that inner feeling of freedom that never ceases to follow us once we've begun this journey.

#workonyourshit is striking the iron while it's hot. It's telling ourselves the truth to our own faces and admitting that we believed in this thing that made so much sense in our lives until now, that we now realize *oh my god*, we were a little bit foolish to believe in for so long (even for 30 seconds). You mustn't do that. You must NEVER judge yourself based on your past beliefs. You are and always have been the exceptional and unique person that you are, the entire time. You always offer who you are to the world and that's the best thing you can do. Even if you've been told otherwise, even if you've *believed* otherwise and you still do. If many thoughts like "I'm so damn far from being on top of it" have come to your mind or come to your mind from time to time, please keep reading this book.

From now on, you are you. From now on, this is the only thing that defines you. Do you realize how much cleaning up we have to do to make simply being you feel so effortless that you don't have to think about it anymore for it to happen? To **just be you**, no matter what, at all times? When I host my VIPs, I like to say that during those 48 hours, we get rid of several layers of shit before we get to the diamond that is us and then all we have left to do is to get to know that diamond. That's also what I'm doing with this book. I'm offering you the opportunity to remove several layers of junk you've accumulated over the years to dig up the warrior in you. The you who, from this encounter with that warrior, will never again let herself or anyone else pretend she doesn't exist. Remember my Santa story. Once you get a taste of *you* and you know she's real, you'll never again be able to act like she's not. And from that moment on, everything in your life will change. Everything.

What I've found, deep inside my vulnerable diamond, is a fucking Rockstar! Just writing it down makes me dizzy. I'm a student/professor in biochemistry. I never thought I'd be a Rockstar one day. I've become, very humbly, a scout for unsuspecting Rockstars. This is precisely and genuinely what I hope this book does for you.

How did I come to this conclusion? This feeling, I felt it for the very first time during one of my conferences entitled "Our unsuspected power over others and over your company's success", which I was giving for the *RMA*[1] in Saguenay. I had already given this conference before and had a wonderful reception from the business-moms who attended. One of my strengths in a conference setting is remembering the names of the participants, their business, their family situation, etc. I adapt my content and anecdotes to make it more compelling and so the participants leave with something constructive.

During this conference, I'm acting the way I usually do, feeling on fire! The girls participate a lot, they answer my questions, share their own experiences and even laugh at my jokes! It's true that I'm super funny at conferences. I've been told this before but this time, it really exceeds my expectations. I come out feeling super pumped! I just gave a conference in goddamn Chicoutimi and I feel like I'm coming out of a show at the Bell Center, one of the biggest concert halls in the province of Quebec with a capacity of 15,000 spectators. You'd think that the Rockstar anchor dug in at this moment, but no.

---

[1] Réseau des Mères en Affaires: A business network for mompreneurs

Not even! I guess the process was a little harder to kickstart this time around! As I leave from there, I start receiving many comments about how awesome I was, how inspiring, how I nailed it; people are thanking me for choosing this career and making a difference in women's lives. Uh, OK! I know, I know, you're reading this and you're thinking that I must have known all of this by that point, that it was nothing new – but no! I know that I make a difference in my clients' lives but the fact that in just one 60-minute long conference, I was able to get them to feel that way, wow! I leave with this incredible feeling in me and I ride on it for a few days. A month later, I'm teaching my module on self-esteem and I take the position of the guinea pig so my students can practice a technique in which I have to define myself as a person and create an anchor. That's when the Rockstar anchor comes up! Me: the coach/nerd/biochemist!

I may be a coach, a speaker, in self-help at that, but it seems that my diamond in the rough is nothing less than a fucking Rockstar! On the surface, it all seems great and pretty simple. One of the reasons women don't pull their diamond in the rough out in the open is fear. Fear of being judged on one hand but more importantly, fear of having to live up to the responsibility that comes with taking on such a role. I invite you to take a moment right now to name your diamond in the rough. How would you name this energy that's inside you right now, that is so hungry for life it screams out from within? As long as it speaks to you, you can call it Warrior, Rockstar, Tibetan Monk, Yogi, it's all OK!

Quick side note. When I talk about a warrior, I'm not just talking about being a fighter, someone who has seen it all, who always gets up on her feet and never gives up. I'm talking about a warrior who doesn't need to do anything. She only needs to *be*. A bell resounded in your ear and you're saying to yourself: "That's all very nice, but how do I do this?" I'll get back to this concept a little later for more explanation because it doesn't come down to "doing" but rather to "being". The big difference for the warrior who IS versus the one who DOES is that when she steps on a mine and it explodes – you know, one of those unpleasant events that happens to us sometimes – she doesn't say to herself, "Oh my god, now what am I gonna do?" Rather, she's thinking,

"Great, a mine just exploded!" She just loves the fact that it did. Subsequently, everything takes its course... Reacting this way to the unexpected may seem like an unattainable level of inner well-being but it's much more accessible than you think.

Second side note, if you've never accessed this kind of energy, don't panic. This too will come out in the next chapters. And that ends the two side notes.

Have you ever heard of the concept that says when you resist or react to something or someone, it's because you're in the right place to grow or expand your world map? Like a reflection of who you are in a mirror that you absolutely don't wanna look at. I like to think that when I react to something in a person's behavior, it's because I have something to learn. Even though sometimes it makes me grind my teeth when someone gets on my nerves, I repeat to myself, "Don't forget, Mari, this person is surely a great teacher for you!" It's not always easy, but they are, so face it!

#rockstarattitude

The thing that makes you react has *something* to teach you, but what you're reacting to is not necessarily related to the *something* in question. Just because you find someone selfish, doesn't mean that you're selfish or that you think you are and it's something you need to work on. Again, the transformation is happening on a deeper level. It's much more likely that you are reacting to what you identify as selfishness in that person because you've forgotten (or haven't learned) how to put yourself first and you don't allow yourself to think about you the way that person regards themselves. If you're accustomed to #workonyourshit, you know that it's connected to something much deeper that affects your vulnerability. If you're new to this, I can tell you that you're not done pulling on some strings and having a bunch of tangled up yarn to unravel. No big deal though. Don't get nervous and don't be afraid. I guarantee you a breakthrough at the end of this. The day will come when you'll be so used to it that you'll see directly what's bothering you in a situation. I'll even admit that swimming on the surface and not talking about the real stuff, when you know the process that leads to transformation, becomes a bit boring.

Another example: your darling mother-in-law says something like "Yeah, it's great that your kids are busy playing outside, now you're free to help out and do the dishes." Many things are happening at that very moment. One, know that she's talking to herself. She feels that a mother with multiple children has no excuse not to participate, according to her own values. Two, it's just her interesting point of view on the situation. It doesn't change who *you* are. And lastly three, if you get into a vicious cycle of thoughts such as "go to hell with your shitty comment", it tells me that you're not honoring yourself because you're giving her power over your thoughts and your inner well-being by the same token. And now, for me, it's a great opportunity to dig a little deeper into why this made you react and take advantage of this to learn more about your inner diamond.

#innerrockstar

Working on your shit when you know there's a guarantee you'll find your inner rock star – I think is a fair deal, don't you?

No matter how much you resist, grumble at me or at life if you prefer, you'll have to do the work to get what you want. And when I say *work,* I'm not talking about killing yourself in order to get there and earn your liberation. All I'm saying is that there's work to be done and it needs to get done, period. Otherwise, you're just going to keep doing what you've always done and attract the same kinds of opportunities you've always attracted. You've been attracting men who need saving, you'll attract wounded men. You've been falling short financially, you'll attract bad opportunities. You're surrounded by people who judge you and don't really like you for who you are... You get the picture, right? It's easy playing fortune teller when I can tell you that if you change absolutely nothing in your mindsets, everything that's going to happen in your life will be the same thing you've always known. Not bad, huh? If you love your life as it is and there's absolutely nothing you want to change about it, then stop. Stop reading these lines and give this book to someone else. Seriously, if you've come this far, the damage is done; your life is bound to get better.

Exercise: My Twenty Qualities

List twenty qualities you possess, along with specific instances in which you've showcased these qualities. Make sure you use a different situation for each quality. Of course, we know that this list is only the beginning of your Rockstar traits.

Example: Generous. I agreed to take my friend's daughter over to the airport.

1.

2.

3.

4.

5.

6.

7.

8.

9.

10.

11.

12.

13.

14.

15.

16.

17.

18.

19.

20

CHAPTER 6

The True Adventure

Before we continue on in a frenzied flow of awareness, each realization crazier than the last, I'd like to offer you a mirror. I don't know if you've yet taken the time to assess yourself and your life since you began reading but I'm convinced that some things have already changed. Indeed, without fully realizing it, your unconscious absorbs what's happening while you're reading. New neuronal connections have begun sprouting in your brain without you realizing it. Isn't that a beautiful thing? You're already part of the adventure whether you like it or not dear because even if you resist and put all this new information in a locked Pandora's box in some corner of your brain, someday, something will create a pop-up and it'll suddenly open!

Often, while we're in the process of making changes, we don't realize the progress we're making as we journey along. Often, the biggest part of my work with a client is showing them how much they've axed in the spheres of their lives and above all, the beautiful awareness they now have of the extraordinary people they are, in addition to their lack of self-esteem being non-existent! Each time, I'm amazed to witness such a magnificent transformation, from caterpillar to butterfly. My god, humans are simply amazing!

Now that we've gone through #workingonyourshit together, I can confirm that we've become pretty close. The more you read, the less guarded you are, the more trusting you become and the more you turn into room temperature butter. When my clients are all-in with the idea of jumping into their vulnerabilities and swimming in them without ever having to plug their noses, I say they're like room temperature butter – easily coachable.

You're ready for the real adventure. The one that makes you dizzy and makes you apprehend facing your worst fears. You should know that the biggest fear I have observed in my clients in the last few years is the fear of succeeding. Yeah, you read that right. Not failure, success. Everyone knows what it is to fail since we're all stuck having to deal with standards and judgments. We've learned to deal with the fears we face when we don't reach our goals; but succeeding is something entirely different. Most of us have been raised to think that we don't deserve things that come easily. From an early age, we're prepared for failure. You know when you're in an environment and you hear: "The most important thing is not winning, but participating. What matters most is to get back up. It's important to enjoy the journey, not just the destination." That all makes you develop resilience and many other exceptional values, it's true, but it also means that your burning fire to achieve exceptional success and experience great things at the level of who you are may not have been well maintained...

The fear of success strikes a completely different chord. I still remember last year when one of my regular clients asked me for an emergency consultation. In the past, we worked a lot on her love life, which had been very tumultuous: a spouse who leaves after the second baby comes along, well let's face it, it's a little rough. She comes into my office with a question, but this time, it's on a professional level. She's been working for several years in healthcare and has recently obtained the position she's always wanted. After only a few months though, she realizes that the working conditions that come with the new responsibilities are far from what she'd imagined and had been dreaming of for so long. It's not working out for her at all, especially because she's working so much that she doesn't have the quality of life she'd like with her children. Now she sees an opportunity to buy a franchise from a banner she loves. She doesn't know anything about the corporate world but she gives it a shot and ends up being selected by the franchisor. She easily comes up with financing and a location. In fact, it's so easy that she comes to see me to make sure she's made the right choice. You see, from the outside, it's obvious that she has a golden opportunity! You might even think, "I'd love to deal with tough situations like that too!" But when you're in the eye of the hurricane, it's not always so crystal clear. No matter how you twist and turn the situation around to make it connect to your mission, the thing that's most frightening is the fear of success.

Changing and achieving success comes with something that not everyone is ready to take on: the responsibility. Once you recognize your value and acknowledge that you deserve success, that you take responsibility for yourself, then who's responsible for the high peaks that you show to those around you? It's up to you. If you give yourself a low value, you don't have to do much to give yourself a high-five but if you're aiming for the top of Mount Everest, you're going to have to do whatever it takes to get there. If, for example, your goal is running an empire versus getting hired at McDonald's, it comes with a different level of responsibility. In your empire, you'll be responsible for the working conditions of your employees, making sure they have jobs, etc. You see what I mean?

From now on, it'll never be the same again. Never again. Once we start our adventure on the path of consciousness, we can't really stop. I say "can't really" instead of "can no longer" on purpose because I have a friend who started a self-help process a few years back and who was doing a major clean-up. Taking care of her inner child who'd been suffering for so many years until she strengthened the confidence of the woman in her. Her process led her to question her relationship. Don't be scared, it doesn't do that for everyone. On the other hand, if you upgrade your level of inner well-being by whatever means, the other areas will tend to want to follow the tempo, inevitably.

For example, when I started working on myself, it wasn't really for me. As you know, my first NLP consultation was in the fall of 2012 when my two-year-old daughter was pulling out her hair. The conclusion of this meeting was that I was depressed and my ex-husband was in burnout. That day, I experienced my first realization. For the first time, a person outside my circle, a complete stranger really, put words to what I was going through, which I was unable to do. The actions I put in place from that day on were not about anyone else but me. I just realized that if I was doing well, my daughters would be doing well too. So, I started this process by taking care of my inner child, building self-esteem and self-confidence, sorting out my relationships, aligning myself professionally and finally, romantically. It sounds like a lot of changes and it means so little compared to what you're going to experience. I didn't really know myself. So as I got to know myself, a lot of changes were made in order to align my life with who I was.

My friend was spring cleaning her life and she got caught up in her own game. At first you think there's only one thing out of alignment. You tell yourself that once it's aligned, you're going to be OK. But if you remember the Wheel of Life from chapter one, if this is your first time going through this process, there's a good chance that several areas will need a little shaking up! This friend, more than a year after she started, couldn't stand the thought of always finding something in her life that was bothering her. She talked to herself (What?! I often do that too!) and decided to put herself in the status quo phase of her process, as she was satisfied with where she was at. She no longer asked herself questions, she no longer made connections with anything, she was enjoying the present. In her relationship, things were fine, and with her children as well; but professionally, she was not able to feel accomplished.

Two years later, she resurfaced in one of my workshops. It was so beneficial to her that she promised herself she would never again close the Pandora's box that contains her needs, her values, who she really is deep inside. It's not always easy to want to do something different when our family and our spouse look at us with their frog eyes, telling us that we have a problem for wanting so badly to be happy, while they aren't doing anything special. Just hitting replay every Monday morning and doing what they're supposed to do. Yuck, yuck, yuck! Guaranteed nausea for me! Not everyone has this need to connect with their life mission, to discover who they really are and to change the world and that's fine by me; but you have to take this factor into consideration. Don't get discouraged by annoying comments. I know, having a spouse who doesn't support your journey is not easy at all... NLP-alize them without them realizing it! Just kidding! As we say, my students and I, we like those Muggles[2] #harrypotterfan. They're a good laugh.

Of course, you may get discouraged at times in your quest for happiness. This can happen when you begin this kind of process. When you decide to choose yourself, to respect yourself, to say no, to receive, to be. You do everything you can to implement the

---

[2] Originating from the Harry Potter books by JK Rowlings: 1) Someone with no magical powers or abilities. 2) Someone who's not familiar with or knowledgeable about a specific subject 3) Someone who's not aware or "woke".

changes you want to make and then it doesn't happen the way you want. In fact, it doesn't happen the way you want *or* as fast as you want. When we put things in place to act differently, this requires us to get out of our comfort zone and oftentimes, a good dose of courage. We become very uncomfortable until we get used to this new zone and it becomes comfortable again. When we experience moments of discomfort and confusion, it means that change is happening. You owe it to yourself to hang in there and stay focused on what you really want. Without that, you will almost certainly revert to your old habits. So don't put too many expectations on how and when the change is going to happen. Trust yourself and the process. One thing is for sure: if you don't feel good, the change is already here. You have already provoked the status quo to get things moving.

One day, I wasn't doing well at all. When my coach asked me why, I told her I was completely out of touch, that I felt like I was in a total void. What I was trying to put into place in my life, I didn't know anyone close to me who had succeeded at that gamble. She laughed and replied, “Since when have you not performed at your best in the void?” Since that day, I have learned to better handle these moments of discomfort because they're my reward for daring to do things differently than ever before. Now I'm chasing after those discomforts because I know that on the other side, there's always something more amazing and perfect waiting for me. I must admit, I've become a #discomfortaddict. Here's what awaits you if #yourenottoochicken. Don't believe me? Good! Test it out for yourself!

CHAPTER 7

Don't Believe Me? Test It Out!

You know, people often show us different ways of doing things through their own life experiences, no matter what the situation may be. They offer suggestions for possible avenues and advise us on what they would or wouldn't do in our situation. Do you have someone in mind? A "know-it-all"? Sometimes, it can get on our nerves a little (a lot)! We know they do it with good intentions because they love us and want what's best for us. It's just that as human beings, we're all unique and every little detail, such as our beliefs, experiences, personality, etc., will influence how each of us perceives reality. We can share our own experience but there's absolutely no chance that two situations will happen in exactly the same way and generate the exact same emotions.

Except if a person (who's full of good intentions) shares their experience with us and from that moment on, it also becomes an existing possibility in our own world map. Do you understand what I'm trying to tell you?

Anecdote

Let's take the example of one of my clients who's a yoga teacher. She was a government employee who turned herself into a yoga teacher and had the aspirations of one day making a living out of her passion. On the day of her last certification class, her yoga teacher told the class that now that they'd graduated, it was certainly not the time to leave their steady job. BAM! She'd just piled on the possibility for her students that it might be difficult to land their dream job as a yoga teacher. Why did she do this? To hurt and demoralize her students? No. She simply wanted to save them from going through what she'd gone through herself, thus avoiding all the hurdles she'd faced and giving them a more positive experience than she'd had.

You may follow the recommended path – and that's OK! We don't always have to reinvent the wheel, as they say. It's like temporarily returning to adolescence... A teenage girl who believed everything she was told her entire childhood. At the age of 13-14, she begins to doubt everything she was taught. This phase is very much a part of developing her own personality. Her baggage includes certain beliefs and values that come from the environment she grew up in. She'll explore the world in order to validate whether or not they make sense for her. Of course, this happens in all sorts of ways that are influenced by the environment around her. Teenagers can explore and feel safe about it. She knows that her parents are open and if anything happens to her or if she has a rather rough experience, someone will be there for her, to listen to her without judgment. She can also explore in a rebellious way because she feels, inside herself, that she has barriers to break down. Lastly, she may not explore. This inaction may postpone the process of learning about herself and lead to feelings of discomfort.

I, for one, have maintained my rebellious teenager side. As soon as someone tells me what to do and how to do it, I automatically try to do the opposite. I'm not telling you that it's a great quality because it often puts me in a state of resistance and it doesn't always have its place. What a waste of energy! It's so embedded in me that on my last business trip, as we were leaving the a la carte restaurant and everyone chose to wait for the shuttle back to the hotel. A friend and I decided to go a different route and walk back to the lobby. Two people out of 30 wanting to walk back, in the dark, with no idea which path to take. We were in no danger, we were in a safe resort, but the fact remains that wanting to go and see what's on the left when everyone else is going right can be a total waste of time. Especially when the option on the right has been tested and retested by millions of people before.

However, the advantage I have is that I can use this rebelliousness in my practice and in my coaching sessions with my clients. I'm able to blow their minds in a very powerful way and create change like never before in their lives! There's always an infinite number of possibilities around what they're going through and I respond with the question "Why not?" every time they tell me: "Yeah, you make it sound so easy but in reality, it's another story..." Why wouldn't it be easy in reality? Life is far from black and white. It's a wide variety of gradients and possibilities. I can assure you that thinking everything is always all black or all white prevents you from having access to all of life's opportunities and even from your full potential.

So if that's your case, if you feel a resistance to trying things out that for you are in the "Been there done that", "Been there, tried everything and it didn't work out" category, I strongly recommend that you be more curious and test out all the options that are available to you. When we want to change our mindset about certain things, sometimes there's a part of us that would like to have some proof in advance that it'll work. To be sure that the choices we make are the right ones, the best ones for us. We don't really feel like screwing up and making mistakes. We want to make sure that the next option is the right one. But you see, the more you step out of your comfort zone and explore, the less you'll need proof because you'll know that every time you listen to yourself and make choices based on YOU, it'll work out! As for me, I challenge life, the universe, by saying to myself: "OK, it doesn't make sense to believe in this or that but it's giving me a light feeling inside, so I'm going for it." Maybe it's influenced by my Aries side! If that's not your way of exploring life, that's absolutely OK! I'm just giving you many suggestions and ideas to open your world map because what happens when we shift our lives into the status quo mode, we only create change out of urgency and not proactively.

For example, when I started creating my NLP coaching program, I used to write my training books and print them myself so that my students would have a book in hand. This saved me the time required for the books to go through the process of layout, correction, graphic design, printing, etc. One day, I was having a conversation with a friend about it and she told me about the resource she uses for her print jobs. I realized that this place was more flexible regarding deadlines and was half the price of my printing company. Yay! So, I changed locations. Until the day an ice storm hit several regions of Quebec, including mine, causing the temporary closure of the printer's shop due to power failure. Once again, I had to find a new solution and ended up sourcing a third printer's office near my home which, lucky for me, had power during the ice storm. How does it get any better? It was cheaper than the last two locations for the same quality of service and product. Jackpot! I'm not telling you that the goal in life is always to pay as little as possible. I like to pay for the fair value of what I buy. I'm not telling you to do extensive research for every single thing you do to make sure you get the best value for your money. What I want here is for you to realize that in life, there are infinite possibilities for everything and that just because once, or even several times, the same scenario has happened, doesn't mean that it'll always happen the same way. When the time comes to evaluate all the different aspects of your life, if you feel discomfort in some of them, you can open up your world map and try out a whole bunch of different things!

Another example of this is in the case of ADHD (Attention Deficit Hyperactivity Disorder). There are a lot of studies, testimonials, well-known personalities who talk about it. What if ADHD was the norm? What if having 42,000 ideas at a time was "normal"? What if it was the norm to be focused on thousands of ideas at the same time, to be disruptive with your energy and what if all the others received a diagnosis of *dullness*? Then we'd have to give them a little something to stimulate them?

The ADHD diagnosis of one of my daughters provided me with mine by the same token. I never took any medication as a child. With time, I realized that I had developed strategies in order to accomplish the many things I've done in my life! Like my famous mnemonic tool "*key glasses purse*". When I have ideas or things to remember, I record messages on my cell phone, I work with an online calendar and another one on paper, I write down everything I have to do so I can free my brain. I'm not at all saying that taking medication is good or bad, I don't have an opinion on that. The only opinion I have is that you should do everything in your power to feel good and succeed in whatever you desire and if taking medication is part of that, then that's what's perfect!

I know, back in the day, children weren't medicated for ADHD and everything was fine... I would be curious though to see the statistics on how many of the kids who were more fidgety than others were successful at getting their dream jobs. Well yeah, there are thousands of career choices out there. Yeah, you can certainly choose several in which you can thrive. I always say, why not try every possible avenue? What do you have to lose and why not give yourself every possible chance?

I've already tried medication for a while and found myself dull; not like myself. I must say that when I tried it, I had already been operating in my own way for more than 30 years! It's true though that if I could be super focused on one thing at a time, I would save a ton of energy for something else instead of having to manage my brain to carry out my projects. But because I also have extra energy, I'm extremely satisfied with the result and with everything I can tackle and accomplish in a single year.

One of my daughters is on medication to help her more easily contend with school. She can now write a half-page text in cursive letters in 30 minutes. Without medication, she writes basically the same text across two pages, in large, almost illegible letters, and it takes two hours. The point is that we tried to help her put tons of different strategies into place before opting for medication. In the end, my main goal was to preserve her self-esteem. So whichever way it can be achieved, that's my ultimate goal.

A person who believes in themselves can accomplish anything they want in life. I'm not here to show you new ready-made beliefs. My main goal is to shake up your existing beliefs and open up your perceptions just enough so that you can choose and believe in yourself and your potential no matter what, despite your barriers. Don't believe everything you read, test it in your own life. Try things out. Experience life, even if it's two out of every 100 people who think that what you're trying is the right thing to do. And even if no one thinks like you do. Trust your intuition, girl!

CHAPTER 8

Hacking Away with the Stroke of a Feather

Most people I meet who've engaged in personal development, counseling or therapy, share with me a painful, intense experience. Those who've never done any introspection, while listening to the journeys of others, can see that it's not a super fun adventure. That's why I understand that many of us are literally scared of diving into introspection because we don't know what we're going to find!

What if I told you it doesn't have to be this way? I've had clients who've been in therapy for years. Yeah, yeah, you read that right, years! Maybe that's also the case for you. Years of looking back at what they went through with their father, their mother, their life experiences, etc. Don't get me wrong, I'm not saying that therapy is not helpful. Well, maybe a little bit, but some people need this kind of approach and that's fine. There are different ways of doing things to accommodate each and every person. Sometimes my clients' years of therapy have turned them into room temperature butter, just for me. And that's great! Still, yes, working on yourself requires some introspection. Again, it doesn't necessarily have to be awful.

The other day, I was at the book launch of "La fille qui flirt avec l'autre monde" (judge me if you want!) and the author, Mélanie Hotte, said something that made sense to me. Specifically, she said that everyone is chasing after their life mission, everyone believes in the importance of being in the zone and finding your "*sweet spot*" but in reality, our first mission should be knowing who we really are. It makes so much sense! How can you understand and connect with your life's mission, the great purpose of your existence on Earth, if you don't know yourself? Knowing yourself and making peace with your past should be priority numero uno!

When people tell me how hellishly painful the "descent into their vulnerability" was, I can't help but think to myself, *But why?*

Why put yourself through that? In chapter ten, where I explain why everything that happens to you and everything you go through is useful, you'll understand that we find great comfort in suffering and feeling as though going through this process is supposed to be tough. Working on yourself, dealing with your issues, silencing your Gremlins in an easy-going way; who do you think you are? And this, as you must be starting to realize, is a conditioning process, among many others, that we've adopted as the proud human being of our lineage that we are. *Beauty is pain, being in tip top shape is pain, you get what you want in life through blood, sweat and tears* and so on. It's the same thing when it comes to grief. Whether it's the loss of a loved one, a separation or other. If you go through it rather easily, you'll hear comments like: "She's in denial. She's not dealing with her emotions, it's going to catch up to her and then it's going to hurt." I understand that it hurts to lose someone; I'm not saying otherwise. But I'm just asking this: Isn't there the slightest possibility that all this could be going differently? Take a couple of minutes to think about all the times you've acted differently from other people; did you hear the type of disparaging comments, usually accompanied by a look that says it all?

If you think to yourself, *I can't do this exercise, I've never done anything differently.* God, I'm glad you're reading this book! Each one of us is unique so if we act like everyone else (a way of doing things justified by all kinds of good reasons), are we supposed to feel WOWZAPALOOZA in all spheres of our lives?

And how do you get out of this sort of waiting room where you wait for something to happen, where you wait to receive a sign from life or the universe in order to finally make the move you've been wanting to make for months, maybe even years? How do we hack away at the most sacred thing in our lives, you ask?

By doing exactly what you're doing right now.

CHAPTER 9

Level Up and Succeed: NO EXCUSES

This chapter is a sudden revelation I had on a Sunday evening in March while I was writing the previous ones. I'm like that, you know! I guess I'm the type of person who, despite her efforts to stay focused on one idea, has a lot of genius ideas that pop up out of thin air. Ringing a bell?

Before I go on, you need to know one thing about me. I'm someone who could be described as a "student". You already know that I did a master's in biochemistry. What you don't know is that since I was a child, board games have been my thing and I love school, science and learning in general. That nerd persona I was given at that time (and that I accepted, by the way, but we'll come back to those infamous role-playing games later) really suited me and I still accept it today. What I'm writing next is a generalization but in my case, it's true. Because I was interested in science and spent all my summers playing teacher, I never acquired great athletic skills. I played dodgeball and was usually the last one picked. I played kickball with my friends from the neighborhood but nothing more. I really would've liked to be part of some kind of after-school sports team. I was a member of my college basketball team for a year but good heavens, I was really terrible at it! I had a lot of heart and I was full of drive and determination, except I hadn't developed those abilities earlier in life.

This side note brings us now back to January 2017 when, as my family was falling apart, I decided to take control over my own health. My life was so bad that I thought nothing and no one could keep me from it. You should know that I'm like most women who've had children. After three back-to-back pregnancies over a five-year period, I ended up 30 pounds over my ideal weight, with poor cardio. New year's resolution: *Doing an at-home workout program.* I was able to work out every day from January to April while also making changes to my diet. I lost 26 pounds, put on 5 pounds and have been able to easily maintain that weight since. What I want to tell you has nothing to do with weight, nor is it a lecture on what is or isn't good for you or your health. Everyone knows that being active and eating well is key. I want to share an observation with you: we're generally more loyal to others than we are to ourselves. We make commitments to our family, our friends, our children more than to ourselves. That's why, on this infamous January 1, 2017, I decided to do as most of us do. Namely, I made a promise to myself to get my health back on track and to get back in shape; one of the most popular resolutions, but also the most commonly broken! Because it's not about *doing* things but rather about taking care of what's behind what we're going through in order to finally shake things up in a lasting way.

I started with the first training video, ready to rock it because in addition to making the kind of commitment that no one holds, I decided to add a little challenge by doing it at home, alone. I don't know if you've ever started physical activity after being inactive for several years but ouch; my body and pride! I wasn't able to do any of the movements that the girl was showing on the screen. Several thoughts were racing through my head, *Geez, I really suck at this!* being the main one... *How could I have let myself go this much? I can't do this. This kind of training is clearly not for me. Why can't I just sit around, lose weight and feel good about myself? Wow! This is painful.* At that very moment, it just didn't make sense to go on this journey. But instead, I decided to believe the lady on TV, who was saying: "It doesn't get easier, you get better." So, I got up every day at 5:30 a.m. to move my body, which wasn't complaining after being forgotten for so many years.

The challenge was not so much doing the exercises and making changes in my diet but working on my mindset. Despite the results I got after only a few weeks, the desire to go a day without working out was still always in the back of my mind.

As a side note, the law of focus states that your reality aligns with your focus. I'm pretty sure it exists under a different name, but I just made up that law! If you decide to focus on what's wrong in your life, that's what you'll get. Issues.

So, among the different training videos, I remember one in particular in which the lady, who, let's be real here, ticks you off a little with her teenage six pack, says to me (yes, I think she's really talking to me but that's something my coach and are dealing with): "Don't quit, you're only quitting on yourself."

This short, simple sentence that instantly captured my attention also made several connections with who I was. The meaning of this sentence echoed with what I was going through at that time and eventually, with my entire life. That lady with the abs of steel was not wrong. If I decided sometimes to sit down and not work out in the morning, who would care? And when that simple sentence struck my mindset, a fiery voice in my head began to growl that all these efforts were for ME! Nothing could stop me from being in tip top shape, especially not me!

You see, we are our biggest limiter when it comes to our goals and aspirations. Due to lack of courage and commitment. Yes, I am telling you that you lack courage at times. The courage to choose you, to put yourself first, to set your limits, to honor yourself. And you already know this. Why do we do this? Fear. Fear of being wrong. Fear of seeming selfish. People around us who don't prioritize themselves in their own lives will tend to judge us if we do, just saying. Fear of succeeding. We're afraid of not deserving all this success.

Brace yourself, I'm about to share a great revelation: we deserve everything we want. Period. No matter what you think of yourself, no matter if you think it's your ego that makes you say that you're freakin' amazing and that you deserve it all, it's the truth and nothing but. Personally, while we're at it, I'd start with a bigger house. You're gonna need it for storage!

At a certain point, I said *Screw it, I'll just sit here and do nothing, no one will ever know.* That's where I was wrong; I would know. And knowing that I was letting myself down, once again, brought me the strength and the colossal determination that allowed me to go on. It was at that very moment that I decided to make a pact with myself. Never again would I let myself down. NO EXCUSES.

And so, I was up every day for four months, sweating like crazy. Then I continued working out, but more sporadically and today, I finally found *my precious*! #lordoftheringsfan As I was saying at the beginning of the chapter, I'm not what we call a natural born athlete. However, I've tried various sports and actually enjoyed it! But when it comes to performance, let's face it, I don't have the highest expectations. I loved dodgeball in elementary school, in high school I signed up for a 48-hour sports event, I took diving lessons at college, then made the basketball team and I've practiced yoga for years. For a nerd, you can't say I haven't tried!

It's only in the last few months that I finally found my sport. After 38 years, it's about time! I got a taste of CrossFit and became addicted to it! You've probably heard of it. My friends had been telling me about it for years and the only thought that came to my mind was: *What the heck?! Who in their right mind would wanna hurt themselves like that?* Sorry for said friends, but it's true. I first tried CrossFit at a networking event organized by my co-VP and I as part of the *Réseau des Mères en Affaires*[3]. I know, I should've known what the event would entail but I thought we were going to a little women's gym with ellipticals and treadmills. When we walked into the

---

[3] Réseau des Mères en Affaires: A business network for mompreneurs

gym, there was just some metal bar set up at the very back. I thought, *Oh no, we're gonna have to follow a trainer up front who does workout moves. Fudge. I have no coordination!* Little did I know what was going to happen to me. Turns out, CrossFit is all about a variety of cardio and weight training. Yeah, it's pretty gnarly. Yeah, it'll always be, because that's kinda of the concept, but what happened to me that day, after the one-hour trial, was that my brain (my Gremlin) was telling me: "Don't do it. Don't get caught up in gym membership payments that you won't hold up. It's way too hard. You're never gonna be able to keep up. You're going to hurt yourself." All the while, my body was screaming: "That's what I wanna do! This is what I've always wanted to do! I finally found an easy way to stay in shape!" Since then, I've been going every other day. Yes ma'am!

CrossFit is the very discipline of NO EXCUSES. When you're in the gym doing your rounds, you don't have time to think about choking. You stand up and do your 50th consecutive burpee. When I come out of a workout, I'm bursting with courage and determination, pride permeating from every pore. I'm proud of living up to the commitment I made to myself. I am proud of pushing myself to the next level. I am proud of outdoing myself in ways I never thought possible in a million years. One month after starting CrossFit, I remember my eyes watering as I did my final sit-ups. It was the first time I was able to complete the whole routine before the clock ran out.

What about you? Do you do the kind of things that you never imagined you'd do and that make you feel proud of yourself? Do you make that kind of commitment to yourself?

Well, sorry for saying so, but I never have failures... Simply because they're not failures but lessons to be learned! The only times I don't reach my goals such as honoring my wedding vows, "'til death do us part", is because I've adjusted my goal or felt there was a better one that would make me happier. Not because it was too difficult. Not because it was impossible. When I decide that I want to accomplish something, in my personal life as well as in my professional life, nothing is going to stop me from succeeding.

I must make a little side note here. I'm sitting in my favorite lazy-boy (I can't believe this is the first time I'm mentioning him! I've used this sofa for over nine years, since before my first daughter was born. I breastfed my children and put them to sleep on this sofa...). Anyway, I'm sitting comfortably in my pajamas and my old pink robe, it's after 11 p.m., I'm wondering how I'm going to write this book, in addition to writing all my NLP training manuals at the same time; and that's when it hits me! If I've decided that I'm going to write a self-help book for women with an urgency to live by July, a deadline given to me by my editor, there's nothing or no one that can stop me. Especially not myself. I know myself well now as an author. I know how much time I need and the conditions under which I prefer to write. So, I worked out the number of weeks I had left before the deadline and how many words I should write per week. I know that I'm a challenge and adrenaline junkie so if at the end of the week, I haven't reached my word count, I'm gonna be able to knock it out in one night!

Do you know yourself well enough to choose winning strategies based on the way you are and how you operate? Do you know yourself well enough to implement actions that will automatically make you shine? Or are you more the random "let's see what happens" type?

You have to realize quickly that, since everything is a choice, you decide what you want, what you get, whether you get it easily or not, and what will or won't prevent you from succeeding.

CHAPTER 10

Hurtful Gifts or "How Is It Helpful?"

Rare are those who've never experienced this scenario: something unfortunate happens, some bad luck. All of a sudden, you feel overwhelmed by a feeling of total discouragement. Not necessarily because it's something super catastrophic but maybe it's the last straw which breaks the camel's back. Like getting your daughters ready for ballet class on a Monday night (why not add a weeknight activity, as if you weren't busy enough with the hectic beat of your daily life?). You realize, after you've dressed them in their snowsuits and dealt with the nagging and they're FINALLY sitting and strapped in the car, that you've lost your key somewhere and you can't find it. I mean, really?! It was in your hand just five minutes ago and of course, when you're about to leave, when you really need it, it's nowhere to be found!

Your Gremlins show up gang-style (at this point, they've multiplied!) and yell: "You're so f****** disorganized, you're such an awful mom, you can't handle a simple key, how can you not have another copy of the damn key, all that rushing back from school, dinner, homework, studying, getting the girls ready, and for what?! For freaking nothing!" And then you call your boyfriend, feeling discouraged, crying a little on the phone and mumbling some nonsense. In your head, you've lost control and it's getting completely out of hand: "Tomorrow I won't be able to drive the girls to school and daycare. I'm going to miss my workday and I'll have to reschedule all of my clients." Your boyfriend says, "Well babe, that key is out there somewhere between your car and the apartment. Look for it!"

I decided (because yes, this is a real-life story) to give up on the idea of getting to ballet class on time. The pressure slowly releases. I end up saving two and a half hours so I can finally do something else with my time and *god,* that feels great! Just when it's absolutely certain that even if I find the damned key, it wouldn't even be worth it to go to dance class, I find my key. On second thought, I was placing too much on my shoulders. I never would have allowed myself to not go if I didn't feel like it or if I was tired; I would never have dared make the decision to not go to ballet class that night.

All this is to say that there's always a use, a purpose, an asset, a learning experience, call it whatever you want, but the fact remains that there's always a gift behind the trials we go through. And it goes even further than that. There is always a gift behind someone's attitude and behavior. In NLP, we call it a positive intention. And it's also true for ourselves. I can hear you say now: *Oh yeah right, when something bad happens to me, it can be useful? I just come away wishing it never happened to me.* What I'm about to explain will, starting today, change everything about the way you see things and by the same token, help you free yourself from certain things that you might be feeling guilty about right now. The truth is that yes, everything in your life, in your system, is useful.

Your system represents everything that is closely or remotely correlated to you. Your family, your friends, your in-laws, your children, your spouse, your financial situation, your work, your stress, your neighbor who mows the lawn at 7 a.m. on a Saturday, your ex, the cashier at the grocery store, etc. This includes everything that touches you and that has an influence, be it small or large, on your mood, your mindset and even on your perception of life!

Let's do a little exercise. Take a situation that's been bothering you over the last few days or weeks and ask yourself: "How is it helpful?" How was it helpful to pick up a speeding ticket yesterday? How is it helpful that my daughter is not sleeping through the night yet? How is it helpful that my coworker is really getting on my nerves? How is it helpful that my spouse doesn't get more involved in the household chores? You can ask yourself this question with everything that's bothering you right now in your life. This means that everything that's affecting you at the moment is useful for something.

You're a smart girl; if the discomfort you're currently experiencing wasn't helpful in some way, it wouldn't be a part of your life. That's when things start to get interesting and the possibility of transformation appears. Take, for instance, my key example; how was it helpful that I lost my key, that I lost my cool? How was it helpful to freak out? Well, it forced me to realize that I wasn't listening to myself, wasn't respecting myself, wasn't allowing myself enough time at all to take care of myself on a daily basis and that I needed to relax that evening.

When I teach my students, who will become coaches themselves, this method of accompanying their clients, it's the most challenging part of their lessons. And it can be even more difficult when you haven't been able to distance yourself, when you're emotionally caught up in the situation while you're trying to find how helpful all this crap you're going through all by yourself is. With only your own feedback. If you're struggling to see how the tough shit you've been going through lately is supposed to be helpful, this is perfectly normal. I did want to share this with you though because it's the only real way to get you out of the vicious cycle of dwelling on old thoughts that always lead to the same solutions and that don't do you any good. It's the only way to get out of your thought process and act differently. Finding the gift or helpfulness of a situation allows our brain to create a new neural connection that will give the experience new meaning. Ideally, this meaning should feel good, liberating, transforming. Once this new meaning is integrated, all the thoughts that no longer make sense are transformed. Instant transformation!

Here are some more examples. A businesswoman comes to see me because she's stagnating financially. She started her business a few years ago and she has reached a plateau in terms of profits. She's tried changing her strategy, working harder, working differently; but as soon as she makes a little extra money, something bad happens (her car breaks down, her roof starts leaking, her ex-partner decreases the child support payments). No matter how much money she manages to generate, something unexpected happens to her and she always just breaks even at the end of the month. She never runs out of money in spite of all these unexpected events but she never has any extra, even though some months break her company's sales records. We talk a little bit about her financial situation and that of her parents (when it comes to money, we always learn by example since there are still no widespread classes on this subject yet to educate us). We come to the conclusion that her parents were neither rich nor poor, they weren't short of anything but they would always break... why yes, even. So, I ask my client, how has breaking even on her budget been helpful? Of course, she answers: "It's not, it's useless! It would be much nicer to have some extra money and not have to juggle at the end of each month." We then started brainstorming on the utility of this situation. What has always breaking even in her budget brought her that was so WOWZAPALOOZA?

Once again, I come back to the importance of WOWZAPALOOZA. When you're looking for the gift behind something, it's super important (I'll never put too much emphasis on this) that it incites that WOWZAPALOOZA feeling inside of you. Understanding that the really difficult thing you went through at the age of four allowed you to be who you are today is not WOW enough for me. It's just not! We're all the result of everything we've gone through in our lives. What I'm looking for is rather a quality, a skill, a way of seeing things that is unique to you. That THANKS to this difficult experience or even to this succession of difficult experiences, you've developed a strength that's useful to you. It's not always easy to find this significance because it often requires going down to the vulnerability level and putting our ego aside. Admitting to ourselves that we may not have made the best choices in the past, that we didn't choose to buy into the best beliefs to help us out, that we did the best we could with who we were, is not always easy. The idea is to always honor yourself in all of this, no matter what the conditions and, most importantly, to not feel guilty about it. How would that be helpful anyway?

Let's get back to my client and her financial complications. She and I are looking for the gift behind this and we find: it allows her to feel safe. You're going to say: "But how can living on a tight budget create a sense of security?" That's what she's always known! Her family has never fallen short on anything, breaking even meant making sure they had enough money to provide for all of their needs. The second this realization happened and took shape on a conscious level, her financial problems were over. From that day on, she never self-sabotaged again and was able to have extra money. You may think this sounds crazy, too simple, too easy or even like believing in magic to believe that simply finding out how helpful this was for her would make everything change for her moving forward. Hold on tight because the magic has just begun.

Another one of my clients came to see me about the impostor syndrome. It's a trend among businesswomen. Everyone goes through this at some point in their lives. Fear of not being up to the task. Fear of not being worthy enough for all the aspirations you have. Fear of not being the right person to make your dreams come true. Who am I to say I'm going to NLP-alize the world? I'm just a girl from the country who studied biochemistry, had three daughters and started her own business. What's so special about me that makes me capable of such a thing? See, the imposter syndrome plagues everyone.

My client comes to me because of this type of questioning, which has been tormenting her constantly. I'm sure you know exactly what I'm talking about. We're pitching ideas, once again, about what this impostor syndrome is doing for her and we get to the revelation point (WOWZAPALOOZA) that it allows her to not be disappointed. In fact, she's protecting herself. By setting the bar low on what she can accomplish, she lowers the expectations she has of herself. It lowers the expectations that others might have as well. She never disappoints. She also realizes that she's far from her full potential and that she's preventing herself from reaching her goals. She's living in the shadow of her life. She didn't know what to do or where to look to understand what was missing.

You see that, no matter what the answer is (there could be several), the important thing is to create meaning for yourself. To create a feeling that translates into words like this: "Ahhhh yeahhh! *That's* why I've been rejected, abused, bullied, etc. It's precisely to develop or give myself the opportunity to experience whatever strengths I have today." I'm aware that the last sentence doesn't really make sense and may seem unreal.

Why does it work that way? Because human beings need meaning. Humans need to know that what happens to us doesn't happen for nothing. We need to be reassured, to know that we weren't just born under an evil star, that we haven't been forgotten, that it's all relevant.

By the way, in case you were wondering, my key was in the ballet accessories bag...

CHAPTER 11

The Unwavering Certainty

Over the years, I began analyzing more closely the process my clients were going through in order to feel Liberation with a capital L. You know, the kind where you understand that you're finally relieved from the burden you were carrying on your shoulders, perhaps without ever knowing why. The kind that makes you say, *Good god, how come I didn't think of that before? How could I have put up with this for so long?* That moment when your whole being becomes truly sure that you are the right person, at the right time, that you're going through the right thing and that until now, everything you've gone through has been to bring you to this very moment.

In the fall of 2018, I was teaching for the first time the very first course I created for my NLP coaching program. There were only three students, one of whom attended via videoconference.

I was stressed out. A lot. I was afraid I wasn't prepared enough, afraid that my workbook wasn't up to par, afraid I didn't have enough content, afraid I had too much content, etc. I didn't have any slides because I was planning to do it in a more interactive way with a whiteboard. I still remember the first three hours; I was speaking with a big lump in my gut and my head kept telling me, "What are you doing here? Who are you to do this? Do you really think you're going to be able to convey how you see NLP?" As you can see, my Gremlin was fully awake!

By the second day, I was already feeling better, my stress lump had decreased slightly. I wasn't standing at the front of the room to explain the concepts. I wasn't even sitting at my teacher's desk. I was sitting with the three students, around the same table, to teach. I can tell you that there were still thoughts judging me: *What are you doing here? It's clear you're not a* real *teacher. It's clear that you're not owning your leadership properly, that you don't have what it takes to do this...*

Obviously, I've seen teachers in action. Whether at university, during my NLP training or even when I was teaching chemistry at the college level.

Never before have I attended a class where the teacher sat at a table with their students. I was judging myself hard and telling myself that I wasn't a good teacher. I didn't meet the criteria of what it means to be a good teacher. On the third day, I started feeling a little more confident and from the students' reactions, they seemed to be enjoying the training and having their minds blown on many levels. I'm addicted to blowing people's brains out. You know when people make that famous "deer in the headlights" expression? In Quebec and other parts of the world, this animal is likely to cross roads or highways in wooded areas. When it does, it may stop in the middle of the road, hypnotized by the headlights of the car coming towards it. A person who's creating new meaning in their mind has the same frozen facial expression when a new connection is created in their brain. A phase of confusion precedes a state of great awareness and liberation.

Seeing my students getting their minds blown like that and their level of comprehension, I began to believe that I was doing a fairly good job by this point.

By the end of day four, I had asked each of them to complete the training by sharing with me the most significant thing they were leaving with. Once it was over, I shared my impressions with them in all honesty and transparency.

I expressed my doubts and questioned myself several times, even though I believed in my program. And then, like a lightning bolt going through my body, I had this feeling of being OK with the human being that I was. Of being at the right time, in the right place and doing exactly what I was supposed to be doing. You know that feeling that everything you've been through in the past was just to get you here, now. To tell you the truth, at that moment, I literally saw my life flash before my eyes and I knew I was in the right place. That's what unwavering certainty is all about. I admit, this situation, told the way I did, sounds a bit weird. On the other hand, there's no better feeling in the world than knowing that what we are is totally worth it and having no doubt about it. Over time, I've found that this certainty is shared by my clients who take part in my VIP training.

Since that day, I've carried this feeling of certainty with me. That overwhelmingly intense feeling, I experienced it 2-3 times in the following year. I made a promise to myself that I would make sure all my actions led to this feeling and confirmed this certainty. I'm making it my mission that you get this too, if you haven't already since you started reading this book.

WARNING
The Gremlin

Some people call them hamsters. You know, it's that feeling you get when your brain can't stop thinking for two seconds. But hamsters are too cute and innocent. Other than spinning in their wheels, they don't do a whole lot. What lives inside our heads and represents our minds is something way more hostile... Like those little beasts that look so cute and cuddly but are actually cunning... I call them: The Gremlins!

Everybody has them but most people don't know how to tame them, get rid of them or ignore their presence. Gremlins live in each of our heads and their role is quite simple: to be the ultimate mental judges.

Their job? Spreading doubt in all matters and at every opportunity.

Your Gremlin is that sneaky little voice you hear when you're about to reach your goal. When you're almost there, he whispers gently in your ear: "What if it doesn't work out?... You're so naive to think you can do this... You're so naive to think you deserve more than what you already have." Ah, that dear Gremlin! With some of my clients, we've even affectionately nicknamed him our inner "bitch". That part of you that literally judges you like it's the day of your final judgment. What you do is never enough, is never OK. This Gremlin is nourished by your fears, by your beliefs, by what you perceive of yourself and the value you give yourself.

I draw a parallel with the film that features small imaginary creatures that wreak havoc on a city: *Gremlins*. They multiply with a single drop of water. Of course! It doesn't take much to feed them. That's why you have to make sure you don't give them that drop of water. Don't let yourself go to that dark place in your head where it can really get out of hand. Also know that they only disappear in the light so you have no choice but to get them out of there and rid yourself of them once and for all!

My advice at this point is to be aware of their existence, to accept the fact that you judge yourself harshly and most likely, very often. Don't judge yourself for that, pay close attention so that you can do something about it right now because you don't want to end up in *Gremlins 2: The New Batch*.

CHAPTER 12

My Vibe, Period

We often hear about energy: "It was all-in the energy, change the energy, etc." What does "the energy" mean to you? It's often a vague, all-purpose concept. For me, what's important for you to understand is that your energy is sacred. Now, what exactly is YOUR energy? It's when you're yourself completely, feeling like you're in total internal ecstasy, grateful to be who you are. I don't know about you, but I can identify this energy when I feel my heart getting huge, when I'm overcome by a very exciting energy and I'm just having the time of my life (the famous WOWZAPALOOZA). Simple, isn't it?

How do we know if what we're feeling is our energy? Take the time to connect with the last time you felt grateful for being the right person, at the right time and in the right place. It's not necessarily on special occasions, as one would be tempted to believe (weddings, births, professional successes, etc.). Often, it's during those little moments when all the planets seem to be aligned in such a way that you feel filled with lightness and plenitude. It's not just about being aware that you're experiencing one of those perfect moments. Sometimes, it fills up your rib cage in an unexpected way. That's the feeling, your vibe.

It can be as simple as that time when, walking out of my manicure appointment, I was sitting in my car, ready for the three-hour drive to Quebec City for a lecture, I remember thinking to myself, *I'm so lucky for this life I'm living. God, how lucky I am to be who I am! I could die today and I would be at peace.* Not in the sense that I *wanted* to die, obviously. You know what I mean?

That same feeling, that same energy, I also felt it in mid-January one evening when I was alone with my three daughters. Immediately after dinner, we decided to go ice-skating and sledding in the park. It was dark when we got there. We realized it was just the four of us, the park was ours! At one point at the top of the hill, just before we were about to go down on two crazy carpets, a cold wind was blowing lightly in the moonlit park and I felt this incredible feeling of pride for being who I am. That was a perfect moment; I couldn't have been happier!

The most intense moment of this kind that I've experienced so far is certainly the time when I was sitting comfortably in my lazy-boy, wearing my bathrobe (typical me), watching *A Star Is Born* starring Bradley Cooper and Lady Gaga. I already knew I would like it since I'm a big fan of chick flicks. Of course, it's the kind of movie that speaks to me too because as you know, for several years now, I've been helping as many women as possible connect with their inner magic and I do all this so that they can live a life that's perfectly aligned with who they really are. So, I knew I would be touched by the story of Lady Gaga's character but I didn't expect at all what happened next.

To give you some context, this notion of connecting and being guided by your vibe, I've been applying it since I read *Being You, Changing The World* by Dain Heer, co-creator of Access

Consciousness. There's a passage where we have to stop and identify the times when we've really been ourselves, without judgment, without questioning.

So, I was having a great time and everything was going great until I got to the part in the movie where Jackson invites Ally on stage to sing with him, a very emotional moment. Normally, I would have shed just a couple of tears but this time, it was like a lightning bolt shot straight into my heart and I started bawling my eyes out. You know when you're crying so hard that there are no sounds to accompany your tears?

As you know by now, I've been working for several years on making my business into an empire. I want to NLP-alize the world, I want to accompany as many women and humans as possible so they can be happy in the life that is theirs. But what you may *not* know is that I also aspire to get really big, to generate millions of dollars with my business and to reinvent the world. I believe in myself, in my potential and I know I have all that it takes. May I remind you, I'm a freakin' Rockstar!

So normally this is what would've happened to me while watching this movie: I would have been thinking that I want that for myself too, being discovered by the whole world. I would've been taken by storm by a war machine of energy and it would've motivated me to keep going and work harder. But then, for the first time in my life, it was different. I was overwhelmed with emotion and thought, *Oh my, I'm here already, that's it, I've done it! I'm this Rockstar that NLP-alizes the world globally.* Seriously, I was shocked by this clear and powerful statement.

Thanks to my NLP program, I have the opportunity to train future NLP coaches in French and English worldwide! I'm FREAKIN' OUT! But even more so because I've realized that I succeeded in reaching my goal!

I was so caught up in my world, creating and writing this training, that it hit me really hard. I hadn't taken the time to realize all of this. I'd just been completely transcended by what Dain had explained in his book. By being myself and believing in myself, I made the choices that tasted WOWZAPALOOZA, I followed my vibe and created my dream life! Without even fully noticing it.

In 2018, I made several choices that changed everything else. Like saying *yes* to Nancy Richard to create an NLP program to offer at her school. Like participating in Alexandre Nadeau's training to work on my beliefs about money. Like enrolling in Kim Grimard's coaching program. Like saying *yes* to Mary, who was offering me the opportunity to coach female entrepreneurs from all over the world – and in English on top of that! All of these choices and many others that I made in the last few years, have allowed me to create the opportunity to be a Rockstar. I created all of this! As they say, everything is in everything! I'll come back to that expression later.

#everythingisineverything

I've finally given myself a life worthy of who I am. That's what it means to be guided by your vibe, period. Don't get me wrong, it's absolutely not about making lots of money or being famous (that too, but that's not everything). Even when I was young, I had the feeling that I was meant to achieve great things on this Earth and to change the world. Today, I'm able to fulfill this mission. I NLP-alize the world y'all, no less! It's possible that while reading these last few lines, some judgments may have popped up. That's OK. You are entitled to your opinion but make sure that these points of view don't relate to the ambitions that you may not yet recognize you have or the fact that you're judging yourself for putting in a lot of effort and not being able to succeed yet.

So remember the last time you had this amazing feeling. Remember who you were with, where you were and what you were doing. If you don't think you've ever experienced one of those moments, that's possible and it's OK. But I strongly suggest that your new goal from now on not be finding a new partner, a job in which you thrive, having an enjoyable family life or making more money. Your new goal is to act quickly to get this feeling fast. Doing the right things, making the right choices to make sure you create it because, as in everything else, we have power over that also.

Do you remember the last time you had that feeling? Your mission, starting today if you accept it (now that I am going to name it, you'll have no other choice because your subconscious will have made that connection), is to make every possible decision according to your vibe.

Now that we've connected to our vibe and had a taste of it, how do we know that the decisions we make will lead us to experience even more moments that bring out that incredible feeling? Good question! Especially if you've never felt that energy before. It's super-duper, ultra simple. Here's the trick I learned from Access Consciousness: does it taste heavy or light? If the idea of making one choice over another makes you feel light inside, it simply means that it's the right decision to make. In my case, all the light feeling decisions I've made didn't make any sense at all with what my head was telling me. Like agreeing to teach my own NLP coaching program that didn't exist five months before. Like committing to a $500/month rent in Montreal to give this training when that's all I was making with my business. Like signing up for CrossFit knowing that staying committed to a gym over a long-term period is a challenge for anyone and that I'm far from athletic. Like paying a private coach and a business coach as a reinvestment when I could be putting my money aside. Like signing up for a five-day Business Mastery in Florida with Tony Robbins, in English! You see? If I'd listened to my head each time, I never would've gotten to where I am right now. Letting yourself be guided by your vibe is so rewarding that it makes you live your life in a way you never even dared imagine.

Did you know that keeping in touch with your vibe can make you lose weight? For example, if you're used to eating a lot of desserts with each meal and you take the time to ask yourself if it tastes heavy or light, you'll have the answer that could lead to weight loss. It's very likely that it doesn't taste light at all and in the end, the need to eat so much isn't yours. Rather, you're lying to yourself, causing an irresistible urge to eat subconsciously for reasons beyond what you're aware of. In his book, Dain talks about a woman who realized that she was eating donuts for everyone in the office instead of doing it for herself. When she realized this, she stopped eating them completely. She listened to what her body wanted. From that moment on, she didn't feel like eating for other people so much and so she lost weight by honoring herself and staying true to her vibe.

So as you can see, staying true to your vibe is key for aligning your life with who you really are. Yes, it's all about the choices you make regarding your love life, friendships, work, health, finances and so on. Oftentimes, we think that most changes are brought about by the really big decisions we make; but remember what we saw in chapter eight: "Hacking away with the stroke of a feather." Change is initiated through micro actions, in the daily decision-making process. This is exactly what happens when the time comes to make heavy or light choices. For example, you've been dating this guy for a while. You're used to packing your suitcase to go to his place every week when you don't have your kids with you. You've been literally living from your suitcase half the time for over a year now. On a given Thursday night, when you just feel like cozying up at home, you decide to stay put. Despite the fact that you are dying to see your sweetheart, this choice of sleeping in your bed and waking up to everything you need to feel good is what tastes light. This is the decision to make in order to honor yourself.

Side note: the importance of our environment cannot be underestimated. Where you're currently living may or may not be temporary. Without being able to explain it, you may not feel comfortable there. Think about it, your environment is what surrounds you at all times. There's your work environment and your personal environment. Our home is supposed to be the place where we feel completely free and not imprisoned. Otherwise, it slowly kills you. I once had a client who was living with a roommate. It was more than temporary, she thought she would stay there for a year at most. Obviously, living with a roommate is not like living with a partner, even if it's a friend. It's proven that in love, we're willing to be more accommodating than in friendship. So coming home to someone who comments on your choice of activities, expenses and environment isn't nice. Where, when, how you should put your things away and how you should get through your emotions isn't what I call an eco-friendly environment for anyone. Imagine if you're having a bad day at work and you can't even go home to recharge your batteries because you don't have a safe haven to call your own...

This client was stressed out in many ways about several aspects of her life. The first step was realizing that she was unable to be comfortable with herself on any level. She was worried about moving again and most importantly, she didn't have the energy but she knew that this was the first move she needed to make because even if she improved her work situation or her romantic life, she kept having to come back to that place where she constantly felt judged for who she was. Sure, I could've told her not to allow her roommate's comments to have power over her, that they're just interesting points of view, that they don't influence her worthiness in any way. Sometimes, we can change our perception of a situation, but action is necessary if we want to choose ourselves completely. It's funny, once she moved into her new apartment, everything magically fell into place.

To move out or not to move out? Sunday dinner at your mother-in-law's or not? Helping your friend or not helping her? Fries or salad? Heavy or light, girl? That's the only question you need to ask yourself to make sure you're sticking to your vibe.

CHAPTER 13

To Each Their Own Female Geniusness

What is ingenuity or geniusness? By definition, it's a superior ability of the mind that makes someone capable of creations and inventions that seem extraordinary. Are we all capable of this? Yes! I'm talking about ingenuity and, more specifically, female ingenuity because I've recently realized that we all have a different kind. However, in order for it to be valued and recognized, what do we compare it to? How can you tell if that's what you're looking at? I had been attempting to define myself for a long time and I couldn't find a comparison. I thought it could be intelligence, maybe creativity, but how do you define it as geniusness? Many women have distinguished themselves in the past by achieving great things, whether it be in politics, science, research, law, family, etc. However, there's still a long way to go in terms of recognizing female geniusness. This is evidenced by a comment I read, from a man what's more, on Olivier Corchia's social media: “It's when things go wrong that women are hired or elected to solve problems. The result: proportionally, women take riskier jobs and are therefore more likely to fail than their male counterparts. And of course, not only are women recruited for impossible missions, but we're not as forgiving as we are for men.”

What are we to do? I'm not complaining or planning a vendetta! Hmmm, well now that I think about it... It's just an observation I made and that many others have made, which brings me to talk about your ingenuity and its place in your life.

There are so many women who have distinguished themselves by their courage, determination and resourcefulness and surely, thousands more who will never be known. These women, for the most part, have made history with their own lives such as Nettie Stevens, an American geneticist, who discovered in the early 20th century that the sex of each individual was determined by their X and Y chromosomes – contradicting men who had been accusing women for hundreds of years of failing to produce a "male heir". Or how about Margaret Hamilton, the computer engineer who in the '60s developed the flight software for the Apollo missions; the woman without whom *man* would never have set foot on the moon.

As I was saying, thousands of women have made a difference in human history despite the fact that it hasn't been made easy for them. Think about it; today, this opportunity to change the world is presented to us on a silver platter. These women have made history, just as you and I are making history right now. You're probably thinking: *Come on, now! How can I be compared to the suffragettes or the first women lawyers, doctors, prime ministers, when doing my 9-to-5 or running my own business?* And here's where I am proclaiming that *yes*, there are still female leaders today who we can admire and be inspired by. But there are also all these women who decide to choose themselves, to honor themselves and make sure that others around them have no other choice but to respect themselves, give themselves greater value and, by the same token, want more for themselves.

Now let's get to the heart of the matter. I think you know that since the dawn of time, we've had inventions, laws, ideas, innovations, etc., based on men. We've been living in a society run by men for a very long time. We've been riding on all these male-oriented inventions. It's true that women have done great things but always by having to pierce through, here and there, a male dominated world.

Did you know that women, in addition to taking our place, have to deal with a tsunami of emotions? Emotions are the most powerful force in the universe. We must manage them and not let them manage us! Both men and women can be under stress. The only difference is that women are different emotionally. We are capable of empathy like no other, we can sacrifice body and soul for others and put ourselves last. Because we have this tsunami of emotions to deal with, we need to develop incredible abilities to master our mindsets so we can accomplish what other women have over the decades. Forty years ago, a woman becoming self-sufficient was a feat in itself, breaking news. Today, all women have access to this autonomy, we have the power over our lives that only men had not so long ago...

It's now common to see women in high positions in politics, business, the military, law, medicine, as family leaders, etc. For the first time in human history, women hold more than 50% of the high-level jobs! And 71% of women with children are employed. The level of stress that women can experience is something that men will never understand. Women have more choice, more freedom, more power; but at the same time, studies show that we're also unhappier than we were forty years ago. Through all this ascension, we have forgotten ourselves along the way and that's exactly why I do what I do. It is my greatest wish that women have all these choices, all this freedom and all this power **while swimming in joy and happiness**. And to achieve that, I'm targeting the democratization of our brain and emotional functions. Once we master the most powerful force in the universe, we can conquer the world.

When researching genius, we practically only find male references; and I'm not even talking about engineering here, where there are more and more women entering the field. I'm talking about people who are called geniuses. Genius is identified, more specifically, in two main fields: scientific and spiritual. To be classified as a genius, one must meet the criteria of both types. Are you following me? These criteria were established thousands of years ago – by whom? By men. Women didn't have a say in it. The two types of geniuses, namely the spiritual genius à la Gandhi or the scientific genius à la Einstein, have no emotional or relational aspects to them.

Women don't think like men, don't do things like men. First of all, the emotional and intuitive side is super present in our geniusness and second, we don't subdivide all the little things into separate little boxes. We're able to connect everything at all times and make connections between all this knowledge and our intuition. Therefore, we cannot plan, organize, succeed, conquer and accomplish ourselves the way men do. It's very important that you realize, if you haven't already, that if you try to reach your goals without exploiting your own geniusness but rather by trying to mimic something you've seen because you had no other references to fall back on, you're wasting a lot of time and energy. It can create a sense of inadequacy deep inside you. Ouch, right?

Making room for your geniusness – how do we do that? It's actually the next step after connecting with your vibe and beginning to make choices based on it. Once you're all set on that, you've reached the stage of harnessing your inner genius. As you know, before I became a coach, I was a chemistry teacher, a scientist. I'm still a scientist, but in a different way. When I was first introduced to NLP in 2012, I didn't know myself at all. I reacted as best I could to the highs and lows of life. In addition to not knowing how to manage my emotions, I often didn't understand why I was feeling the way I felt. Of course, I've changed a lot since I began my journey with NLP but most of all, I've discovered who I really am.

To be able to bring your geniusness out of the closet, you have to start by knowing yourself inside out. Then comes some process of liberation, awakening and claiming responsibility if we want to not only connect with our geniusness but also to be able to exploit it to the max! The idea is to take our greatest strengths and bring them to the forefront so that as many people as possible can benefit from them. We may also have to get over our impostor syndrome. For example, if you have a business, you don't always have to be all over social media but you have to know what you're awesome at and yell it out to the world. Can you feel a little bit of gremlinian stress rising when I say that? "What if people don't recognize that I really have this talent and that it makes a difference?" "What if people don't like me and reject me?" "What if people judge me and start saying that my service or product isn't worth crap, that I'm a fraud?" Do you see that there's a very fine line between saying, "I know what I'm worth, I'm going to shout it from the rooftops and change the world," versus "Who am I to think I can make a difference in people's lives? I'm just a simple human being who does what she has to do." Even if you don't have your own business, you will have this internal rhetoric to overcome, until you get to the: "No matter what people think, when I'm myself, I inspire people so much that I make this difference in the world" phase.

You get to know yourself, you get rid of all the junk you've been carrying around for years and unleash your inner genius! After many years of trying to understand my deep functioning (less than ten, by the way!), I'm at a point where I have mastered my geniusness. I'm able to activate it at all times, I create the optimum conditions in all spheres of my life in order to be able to use it. My geniusness consists of connecting with the person in front of me. I want her to feel understood like never before. I want to put what she's feeling and experiencing into words, something she hasn't been able to do. I throw her into her incredible inner beauty. I want her to feel confident like never before, to have the certainty that she has great value and that she's capable of anything. Sometimes, whether you want to or not, accepting your geniusness, your light, your glory, your stature obviously comes with taking full responsibility for yourself. Depending on where the person is in their process, they will get there at their own speed. And it will take as long as it takes, it's really not important because at the very least, I've set things up. Setting things up is also one of my great strengths of geniusness – but that's not the subject of this chapter, so I'll come back to that later.

CHAPTER 14

The Roles We Play

I recently read that we all have many roles in our daily lives – and I'm not even talking about our role as a woman, mother, mommy and lover. I'm talking about the roles that we assigned ourselves when we were young, that we chose to play, consciously or not, and that we continue to play to this day. One spring when I was about 38, while I was out riding my four-wheeler in the snow, it clicked! As you know, I loved playing board games when I was little. From the age of 5 or 6, I adopted the role of "the nerd", the bookworm who did her homework, who loved going to school and who, since elementary school, had the desire to be the best and always outdo herself. I was the first, on both my father's and mother's sides, to go to university. School was my mojo. While I was completing my master's degree in biochemistry, I was also in a program to become a college level teacher. After completing those programs, I did a certificate in business management to acquire the necessary knowledge to help my then husband in his organization. I'm a "learnaholic"! I have a curious nature, a passion for knowing everything and understanding everything. So I've continued playing this role, even today through my teachings and research on women's ingenuity and geniusness. The trouble with this role is that I'd also chosen to be the nerd who isn't handy.

I don't know if you've noticed but I put a lot of emphasis on the verb "choose". I know very well that in order to choose these roles at a young age, they must first be suggested to us in our environment or reflect a need so we have no other choice but to play them. It's completely intentional because for me, no matter what the reason is for playing the role of nerd, jock, reject, etc., we did it because it would benefit us eventually somehow, in some way. Remember, no matter where you come from, what you've been through or what you've done, everything is within your responsibility. It's the same for those infamous roles we play.

So, I didn't really fix things and I had difficulty managing on my own. I was dependent on others as soon as it involved a physical task and that day, in the middle of the snow trails at the sugar shack, it hit me like a brick. I didn't want to play that role. I wanted to be a nerd who can take care of herself. So it was then, while in complete control of my ATV, that I realized how much strength I had in my arms; that I was perfectly confident and in control. I asked myself: *Why is it that just before leaving for the ride, I couldn't find the start button?* My brother had explained it to me but once I was on the four-wheeler, I couldn't see anything. I had to go back to him with my "I don't get it" voice so he would come press the button for me. Gosh, I felt stupid. Hear me out here. I'm not at all suggesting that you have to understand and know everything or else you're stupid. What I mean is that he'd explained how to do it and I realized just then that I, voluntarily, hadn't grasped it so I could depend on someone and play my role as a girl who wasn't manually resourceful. Intense, huh? How many roles do you think you play in your daily life?

What's great is that once we become aware of our roles, we can decide to stop playing the ones that don't suit us anymore – and that's it! So I realized all of this and looked at my life in retrospect regarding that role, all the while having the time of my life on a dirt road. Incidentally, since living alone after my breakup, I've been in charge of everything my daughters and I need. I make sure that my car is in A1 conditions, I shovel the snow, I put frames up on the walls, I do it all! Upon becoming aware of this, a huge feeling of empowerment and confidence came over me. I didn't want to play the role of a hands-off nerd anymore!

I know I have many other roles in my repertoire: the girl who makes people laugh, the girl who triggers people's awareness, the girl who links everything together, the girl with a phenomenal memory, the girl with great empathy, the sensitive girl who cries with her clients and so on. I love all these roles and consciously decide to play them with panache!

Here's the case of one of my clients (are you like me, the kind of person who's become addicted to all these anecdotes?!). As far as she's concerned, all is well with her children and her spouse but she's trying to find herself professionally. She's in her thirties and she's bouncing from one project to the next, never knowing if she actually likes what she's doing or not. Obviously, like all of us, she has responsibilities and wishes to do more than her share in regards to the household income and also be financially independent. I start asking her questions about the kind of professional goals she would like to achieve. She hesitates for a while and tells me that she'd like to reach the $100,000 mark this year with her business.

When I ask my clients what they really want, oftentimes they don't even know. In fact, their gremlin prevents them from knowing. Do you remember the job of the gremlin that lives inside all of our heads? Making sure we stay in our uncomfortable comfort zone and we don't have thoughts of ambition and aspirations that would put forth the person we really are! So her gremlin is doing a great job: "Why would you ever hope for something better or different? Your parents have always been there for you. You have no reason to complain about your life. You have no reason not to feel happy and content right now. And for goodness' sake, don't you dare desire to make more money. Who do you think you are? What will people think?" Yes, I know the speech of each of my clients' gremlins very well. That's why I always use the strategy of extreme exaggeration to help them rationalize their thoughts. For instance, when she talks to me about money, I always respond using very high numbers, talking about making millions of dollars in my business. It makes it easier for them to live with the idea of wanting to make $100,000 that year. The client quoted above even went so far as to tell me $150,000. Yay!

And of course, this statement was accompanied by its load of justifications: "You know, when I make this money, it'll allow me to provide my four children with a better quality of life. It'll allow me to give back and make a difference." In no way was she ever going to tell me that this would allow her to take care of herself, spoil herself and shine even brighter. Certainly not! It was only after a few minutes of discussion that we realized she had always played the role of the adult in her life. Since she was very young, she has adopted the role of the good, quiet girl who does what she's told, who behaves flawlessly... And her parents never demanded that of her! They truly accepted her for who she was; *she* chose that role. In fact, we're always the ones who choose, consciously or unconsciously. And choosing to play the role of this good little girl resulted in the fact that today, she couldn't be herself in her own life. She didn't want to play that role anymore; she wanted people to see the funny, extroverted and somewhat eccentric person she is! Do you think that by consciously choosing not to play the role of the good girl anymore and taking on the role of the eccentric person changed something in her finances? Absolutely! And how did I know it would when we were talking? It's not because I think that good people don't make money or that eccentric people necessarily do. It's because she came to me for a consultation in my virtual office to tell me about it. That to me already means there's likely room for improvement; otherwise, she wouldn't be there. Never underestimate the importance of what you're feeling.

I once offered a free 30-minute "discovery" call through my Facebook group. Several women wrote in to tell me that if no one was taking the available spots, they would take them – but that they were doing fine so they preferred to leave them to women who needed it more... Oh, boy! Let's get something straight right now, you and I! First of all, everything you're going through, even if it seems less serious to you than what your neighbor is going through, who cares! If it makes you feel bad, it's worth talking about and making time for. Second, can we agree that you're the worst judge of whether what you're going through is significant or not?

We're usually the worst person to help ourselves see things differently. I often tease my students when one of them explains the why and the how of what she's going through. I remind the others that we must not listen to whatever it is she's saying, at all! On top of becoming an expert on her own problematic because she has overanalyzed it, she thinks she has applied the right techniques and reframings on herself. I'm convinced that she has not.

And in my client's case, why was I 99% sure that updating her roles would have a positive impact on her finances? She had gotten to know herself and what she really wanted. Automatically, there would be an influence on her future choices as well as on her business earnings. I'm telling you now and I'll say it again, choosing and listening to yourself (I'm talking about your intuition of course, not your gremlin) is always a winning formula!

Now I can hear you all say: "I want another anecdote, I want another anecdote!" Since I'm attentive to my beloved readers, here are two more examples to help you understand, integrate and illustrate the concept of role playing.

Laura came to see me to work on her impostor syndrome. As you may have noticed since you started reading, the majority of the reasons why people seek counselling are low self-esteem issues and undervalued self-worth. The impostor syndrome is no exception, since it comes with its gremlin and its now well-known speech: *Who are you to think that you can do that?* Laura tells me about her aspirations and that every time she puts everything in place to achieve great success, she starts to self-sabotage. She forgets to do several tasks that she had taken the time to list months before to make sure that it all went perfectly! Self-sabotage, procrastination, anxiety attacks, you name it – just to keep things from being easy. One of the realizations she made was the importance of her inner child in her life and the associated consequences of that. For one, it made sure her parents could interfere in her children's education. Let me explain. Laura lacks so much self-confidence that she often asks her parents' opinion before doing anything: buying a new car, renovating her house and raising her children. This creates too much space in her life for her parents. Let me remind you that a person is not just a behaviour. So the question that should always come up when someone gets on your nerves is, *What am I doing to attract this kind of behaviour?* Yes, you do have power over another's behaviour and yes, you're an incredibly smart woman so, what in the hell are you doing, allowing that to exist in your life?

The other realization Laura made is that, ever since she was very little, she had been playing the role of the one who lacks self-confidence and above all, who always needs others. In no way could she do it alone. And how did she end up playing this role? Partly because she came from an ultra-rational family where emotions didn't exist. Laura was super-emotional and sensitive to what other people were going through. It was reassuring to justify and explain who she was by taking on the role of the one who always finds herself in difficult situations; the only logical explanation for all this! What impact do you think this had on her business? She was successful nonetheless, considered to be an expert in her field and everyone was obsessed with her! But oh, the amount of energy it was costing her to fight this role! I can hear you say: *Yeah, but she was succeeding anyway, so the rest doesn't matter!* Wrong! Since we got rid of some of the different roles she was playing and she realized that she no longer wanted to play the girl who always needs others to succeed and get somewhere, no more anxiety attacks, no more self-sabotage and most importantly, no more going through all this alone and always taking on all the blame. She's been able to surround herself with the right people so that she can be more successful on all levels. This is a much better scenario, don't you think? From my perspective, it sure is!

Another important thing to consider when talking about roles is that they're reassuring for some people. For example, say you realize that you're playing the part of someone who's not sure of herself, as in Laura's case. You decide that you no longer want to play that role. Well, it may have been reassuring for certain people around you to know you were playing that role. Now you're probably like, *What the what? There are people in my circle who feel reassured by my lack of self-confidence?* It's not so much that they're reassured because you don't believe in yourself; it's more because it's familiar to them, so if you change this role overnight, it changes your system and by the same token theirs. What's more, maybe your role justified one of *their own* roles. Think about that for a minute. If you play the part of someone who lacks self-confidence, you'll inevitably have people around you who play the role of cheerleaders: *Let's go, you can do it! You got this, don't give up, you can do it! You're the best, honey!* And this role, whether you like it or not, has been highly gratifying for them. This is all without bad intentions and most likely subconscious. It's gratifying to think that despite everything our daughter or our friend has lived through, we've always been there for her, no matter what!

So, say from now on you decide to stop playing the role of the one lacking self-confidence and decide that no matter what, you'll never doubt yourself again. Then you're forcing them, from here on out, to redefine the roles they play, without them ever *wanting* to change. No worries, it's always for the best; but there's a good chance it will trigger reactions from those around you. Remember, it's not because they don't want you to believe in yourself. It's simply because, temporarily, it takes them out of their comfort zone, they lose their bearings and that pushes them to redefine themselves. Trust the process.

Roles and Relationships

These infamous roles may seem irrelevant but we forget how much they can define the types of relationships we're in. For example, with people we haven't seen for a long time, we have as a reference these roles that connect us. Like an older brother who keeps mentioning his little brother's fear of needles... He's 35 years old today and has been able to deal with this fear for several years now. Like each time you're in the presence of your mother and one of your roles presents itself again when you're no longer playing it. This is normal because your mother may deliberately bring you back. It makes sense; that's the way she's been defining herself in your relationship. It's like if you had been playing as a hockey goalie since birth. All of a sudden, without warning, you decide you don't want to play that position anymore. You haven't taken the time to mentally prepare everyone that you would no longer do it. You're already going through the process, you're not going to talk in detail about your barriers, what you're working on, etc. So, when you show up to people and they don't understand why you don't want to play hockey as a goalie anymore, their first instinct is to remind you how good a time you had in that role – all the while, trying to put a goalie stick in your hands, a helmet on your head and skates on your feet.

You might also find that after putting one of your roles away for some time, all of a sudden – BAM! You find yourself playing it again without ever seeing it coming. It's OK. As I was saying, the people around you haven't made the choice to change. They now need to redefine themselves in light of the changes *you've* initiated. They don't know it yet but it's for the best, for you *and* for them. This change is meant for you to be happier. Also keep in mind that their intention is not for you to be unhappy. They're just not aware of what you're going through and are reacting to being out of their comfort zone. That's all.

As you can imagine, this can also affect our children. Just as we began taking on many of our roles as children, our precious offspring are doing exactly the same thing as we speak. No need to panic: *Oh Lord, what am I doing to my kids?* It's pointless. The goal here is not at all to make you feel guilty. Your children each have their own life path. I agree that we don't want them to experience horrible things and we want to spare them from the hardships we've been through. But the reality is that our children have to live life for themselves and the only thing we can do is offer them a rock-solid example of great self-esteem and confidence. I mean, if just by watching us, they learned about all the benefits that choosing yourself on a daily basis brings, a batch of adults in the making is already much better off.

How can this be reflected in the lives of our children? It's very simple. Let's take the example of my client Suzie, who has five children. By the way, having multiple children doesn't make things any different because there are thousands of roles we can play. One of Suzie's children can't take away all the possible roles from any of the other siblings. Suzie is a savvy entrepreneur who performs very well professionally. She's a determined, dedicated woman who succeeds in virtually everything she takes on. When you're raised in a system where performance is present, as a child you can choose to perform. It usually happens without you realizing it. You can also rebel because it viscerally contradicts with who you are. Not because you have something against performance but it's not part of your core values. Except, you were born in a family where performance is queen. I'm not even trying to justify where this value came from in the system because clearly, it was useful to one or both parents to survive at some point in their lives.

Suzie, my client, comes in for a consultation and tells me about her daughter, her oldest who's 10 years old and highly bored. Nothing interests her. No matter what activities Suzie and her husband offer, their daughter prefers to stay isolated and play video games. She tells me about her other children. Her oldest excels in sports, her second performs well in school, her third wins awards for exemplary behaviour and her fourth is a science whiz. What does her youngest have left in terms of roles to adopt and define herself with so she can be recognized in the same performance standards as her siblings? What if she doesn't want to choose from whatever choices she has left? Aren't there infinite choices available to her? Who said it wasn't OK to not have performance as a core value? Do you see that if this 10-year-old girl chooses to play a different role in this family, she risks being judged (she subconsciously thinks so because she's unable to see other possibilities) and not recognized for who she really is? These aren't things that are said explicitly and parents generally don't even put pressure on their children to perform. Children learn from their parents' behaviours and if it's the example they've had since birth, it can be difficult at that age for them to envision other ways of doing things.

What if she wants to be an artist? What if she wants to be a hard-core gamer? Is there room in her family for these roles? Wouldn't it help to give her interests in drawing and video games some attention and recognition? The father is actually a fervent gamer but because it was important to him, in his set of values, that his children didn't spend all their time gaming, an interest in games was seen as not OK in their system. This child had been seen by a psychologist, a doctor, etc. and nothing had been identified. I strongly believe that she was reacting to the system and that if her parents became aware of it and changed some things, everything would improve.

A few weeks after her consultation, Suzie told me that she and her husband were paying a different kind of attention to their daughter's interests. Her husband played video games with her. Also one day, during a casual conversation in the car, the topic shifted to those who draw the graphic designs for video games. Their daughter was very excited to hear about this. It's not that we already want her to determine her career. The goal is for her to find an interest in something, so that she has passions and can discover herself through them.

CHAPTER 15

Le Mal de Vivre or The Pain of Living

Here I am, on a three-day weekend in May with my sweethearts and, let's keep it real now, I'm in a really shitty mood. You know that feeling that comes from God knows where, which I affectionately call: being in a #emotionallyshittystate. No matter how hard I try to get in a better mood, nothing helps. Meanwhile, I'm super happy to be spending these three days off with them. I particularly love those moments when we're not in the frenzy of our daily life and the sleep-school-work routine. You can do whatever you want, go to bed later, etc. I'm the type to blow up a mattress and camp out in the living room, build a fire in the chimney and roast marshmallows. So my tribe and I decide to go on a bike ride to a park that we've never explored before. The truth is, I know there's a convenience store nearby where they sell banana flavoured popsicles and I also want to see if my girls are able to bike all the way there from home. In case you haven't heard, banana flavoured popsicles are life! This kind of spontaneous activity is totally in my comfort zone. Once I get there, the girls play in the modules and I use this opportunity to practice my English. I had everything planned, including water and snacks. When it comes to my daughters, the apple doesn't fall far from the tree; they'll adapt to pretty much anything. Lunchtime that day consisted of a gourmet menu of watermelon, cheese popcorn and sour candy. Those were supposed to be snacks but since we were having so much fun when lunchtime came, we adapted! We realized after a few hours that we weren't done playing so we headed to a second park. We're like the Energizer Bunny! Just five minutes after arriving at our second location, I realized there was a BMX track located just behind the swings. A family is watching their four-year-old daughter practice jumps on her big girl bike. I mean, whaaat? Crazy, huh?! I holler at my girls to come and see this and, obviously, they wanna give it a try. Their mother's daughter, indeed! I'm on rollerblades, a little detail I forgot to mention and which makes the story that much more goofy.

We arrive at the foot of the hill we have to climb before starting the circuit, which from close up now seems much less suitable for my three athletes with stabilizing wheels... My daughters beg me to try it anyway. After all, the girl who's already doing it is younger than they are, so why not!

I quickly realize that I'll have to assist them more than I thought in the beginning. I take off my rollerblades and find myself in the wet sand with my socks on. Both of my oldest girls are ready at the top and are waiting for me, very excited... Oh dear; all of a sudden, I'm not sure if it's a good idea... My second oldest goes first and falls on the very first hump (out of 28). My oldest decides to go anyway and makes a nasty landing worthy of YouTube videos, at the same spot. We stayed on the BMX circuit for almost an hour, where I spent most of my time trying to catch them as they lost their balance and running in the sand through the slopes. I managed to convince my baby not to try so she was having fun running among the bikes. Of course, it ended in tears with bruises and almost broken wrists. Not only that, they still had to ride their bikes back home. Yes, I can hear you judging me all the way over here, from wherever you are! Judge girl, judge! Then we took it easy. Duh! We went back to the same park just before it got dark but by car that time.

The point is that I love doing activities with my daughters that are out of the ordinary and unplanned but despite this fun adventure, I had an uneasy feeling inside me that I couldn't shake off. I did my EFT, talked to my friends, shared all my thoughts and feelings with my coach, but nothing helped. It was strange; somewhere between *Oh my god, I'm so lucky, I really have everything I want in life* and *#FML...* kinda hard to follow!

I decide to go to bed early to put the odds in my favor and have the privilege of waking up without an alarm. In spite of this, I wake up on Sunday morning with the same dark-souled spirit that still haunts me. I decide to keep fighting. I get my princesses ready and head out to the CrossFit gym. The girls are great; they let me work out without interrupting me. The workout feels awesome. That day, it's especially demanding in terms of energy and effort. A heavy ball to throw with all our strength to the wall and then to the floor... I needed to let out some steam and it was perfect. I come out of there feeling pumped up so I tell myself that I'm finally going to change my mood and be able to enjoy a nice day with my daughters. Nope. I'm back home, feeling just as poorly deep within me. My oldest gets invited to a friend's house. I decide to listen to myself. I put on a movie for the other two and I lie down for a little power nap. I'm having a hard time sleeping despite the heavy fatigue weighing me down. After vegetating for an hour, I change my mind and decide to kick myself and get into action. I power through making dinner, doing dishes, the laundry and even the four beds get made! At this point, I'm faking being on fire. I'm hoping *I fake it 'til I make it.* I'm faking so hard, I feel like I'm about to catch on fire! Aside from the fact that my apartment is starting to look like somewhere liveable, nada. Nothing on the mood side seems to be getting better.

You see, feeling like this can happen to anyone. Even to me, who is a coach, who has a coach and who's been in this personal growth process for several years now. It's true that when bad things happen, it can make us go through some really tough times and emotions. But experiencing the pain of living while our life is going great is pretty rough. And that was genuinely my case! OK, you're going to tell me that if I was carrying this feeling with me, there had to have been something that wasn't quite right and it was just escaping me at the time. My health was good, my business was good too, my family, my finances, my children, well, my life was great! I was trying to review and rationalize everything and it clearly wasn't working. That's when my coach made me realize that there was a good chance this whole #emotionallyshittystate didn't belong to me. Now I can hear you say: *What do you mean it isn't yours? You were the one going through it!* I don't know if the word empath, which can be translated as hypersensitive, means anything to you. Basically, it defines a person who's very sensitive to the energy and emotions of animals and people, both in people who are close to them and strangers. Empaths will often internalize other people's feelings without knowing it and interpret them as their own. I know that not all human beings are like that but if you are open enough to read this kind of book, I can already confirm that you are one of them. What this means is that 95% of the emotions we feel don't belong to us!

Can you imagine? At first, I was skeptical about this theory. I was in resistance, mainly because I help people on a daily basis better deal with their emotions and now I was being told that it didn't belong to them anyway! Yet, I have to admit that each time my coach asked me if what I felt belonged to me or not, the very strong feeling that it *didn't* was coming up from inside me – and I immediately felt lighter. And we don't even need to know who it belongs to. By simply realizing it, as if magically, the heaviness disappears!

On that infamous weekend in May, I tested this theory and it more or less worked at first. It wasn't my first test. Part of me was saying that's what it was and I should just let go; but another part of me wanted the heaviness to stay. It's a strange observation, right? You'd be surprised how many people voluntarily and subconsciously want to stay in a certain heaviness. Whether it's because that's what they know, whether it's because they're looking for sympathy from the outside world or anything else – the fact remains that when they're going through something, there's a greater advantage to staying in that situation than getting out of it. #truestory. Which means they're nourished by being the victims of what they're going through. That's what I call "victimitis". And I really think it would be very beneficial for all of us to realize that it exists and that we get "victimitis" every once in a while. We're all members of society so it's high time that everyone came out of their caves!

Monday, our third day off, *I DECIDED,* no matter what the reason was behind this pain of living, that I wouldn't remain in this state. You read that right. I made the choice that, despite the thoughts and beliefs that kept me in this state, I was choosing that it didn't belong to me. I know, I know; easier said than done. But as I told you, part of me knew that my mind was deliberately staying in this state for a reason unknown to me. So I could make a different choice. We all can, always. I too sometimes go through #emotionallyshittystates. The only difference, after all my years spent getting to know myself, learning all my tools and putting them into practice, and above all, not going through these moments alone, is that these states are less frequent and 10 times shorter. Before, this kind of episode would have plagued me all week. What am I saying, it would have persisted for several months! Taking a break, taking a step back and changing your perception really speeds up the process.

You should know that the morning before my breakthrough, I broke down. Yes, I broke down and cried in front of my daughters, who rubbed my back for a little bit. I have this belief that as a mother, we're always role models so showing our children that we can falter and feel sad, that we have real emotions, is perfectly healthy. Showing this vulnerability is also showing them that being a woman means taking action towards achieving your goals and that on this road, there may be times when it's more difficult than others. Showing my daughters that it's OK to have emotions, that it's OK if we don't always understand what's happening to us but that the important thing is to always believe in yourself no matter what, is an amazing lesson. Sure, I didn't go through this rather difficult weekend for that purpose but since it's happening, they now know that I'm no more or less because of this tough experience. I am who I am and I dance to the joy of being that person more and more each day. I sincerely hope that they're already learning to respect and love the incredible human beings they are. My daughters are already exceptional. They care about and love others and already seem to wanna make a difference in this world. My goal is far from being unable to manage my emotions to the point where my own children find themselves paying the price. I believe that if we each take responsibility for our own happiness, our children will be happy too.

We ended the day joking around, playing on the Wii and then I started dancing. That's when my oldest said: *See Mom, that puts a little joy back in your heart.* We are exceptional women. It's normal for us to ask ourselves thousands of questions and always want to make sure we're doing the right thing, what's best for the situation and for who we are. You know, the kind of women who wanna make a difference. So that's what happens when we start to open our consciousness; it comes with this kind of mini crash. We know we're doing everything right and we know that we *are* everything right. But then again, sometimes we carry this painful feeling that we're not enough. You have to get through that phase. A phase which will surely come back randomly, like on that wonderful weekend in May. I say wonderful because after these three intense days, I once again realized many things. I learned to understand myself better and above all, I put an end to this strategy that had become very limiting for me. Namely, willingly staying in this dark mood in order to get sympathy from others. I mean, what a restrictive strategy indeed! Especially when you don't tell anyone that you're not feeling so good!

While reading this chapter, maybe you've been thinking, *Oh my god, this happens to me so often too, having this mood that comes out of nowhere!* or *She's tired over just that?!* No matter what went through your head as you read these lines or any of the lines in this book, they're only observations guided by your perception. In other words, these are just interesting points of view. What's important to realize here is that taking the time to observe these different thoughts will enlighten your beliefs and most likely, lead you to understand what's preventing you from getting what you want out of life. These interesting thoughts and points of view speak of you, dear! It doesn't matter what you think, even if it makes you feel good at first and then you immediately feel bad for having this type of judgment – who cares! It's not a big deal. Everyone judges and the fact that you judge yourself for judging shows your great capacity for introspection and desire to be a better version of yourself. Just stop this devilish habit right now and put your energy somewhere more helpful and meaningful. Observe the way in which your judgments speak of you. For example, maybe when you read that I had a meltdown you thought, *Really?! That girl is pretty, sweet, smart, healthy, has healthy kids, can afford to go to the gym, even has the determination to go consistently, why does she have le mal de vivre?* Take a couple of minutes to observe these thoughts because they say something about you, how much you value yourself, your goals, what you'd like, what you think you deserve or don't deserve. My friend, this kind of introspection is what living in your vulnerability and facing it is all about!

EFT

According to Gary Craig, founder of EFT (Emotional Freedom Technique), this technique is the emotional version of acupuncture without needles. He also calls it "tapping". I first came across EFT during one of the seminars I attended with Alexandre Nadeau. Since the spring of 2018, I've been using this technique every day in order to free myself from all the emotions and beliefs that prevent me from reaching my goals.

The basic principle of EFT is that it focuses on the emotion to eliminate the cause of pain (physical, mental, emotional). It's possible to eliminate the emotional problem at a deep enough level that physical healing can follow! If the flow of energy along our body's meridians fails to do this well, our health suffers. If the meridians are stimulated by tapping them with your fingertips, this properly restores the flow of energy by sending signals of well-being to your unconscious mind. This action must be done while at the same time saying out loud whatever it is that you find difficult at that moment. Then your unconscious mind registers a well-being sensation and gets rid of the negative feeling connected to what you're going through.

People with intense emotional problems have seen them disappear. Sometimes it only takes a few minutes to release an emotion that's been with us for years. So, as soon as you start dealing with these emotional issues and you actually resolve them, the physical manifestations disappear.

What blocks the flow of energy the most is the way emotional problems and traumas from our past are registered in the body. EFT gets to the source of the blocking and treats all its side effects like addiction.

I used the technique I learned during the training and combined it with typical phrases found in the Access Consciousness approach. Here's a diagram of the eight points that Alexandre uses in his sequence and that I also use (although there are several others):

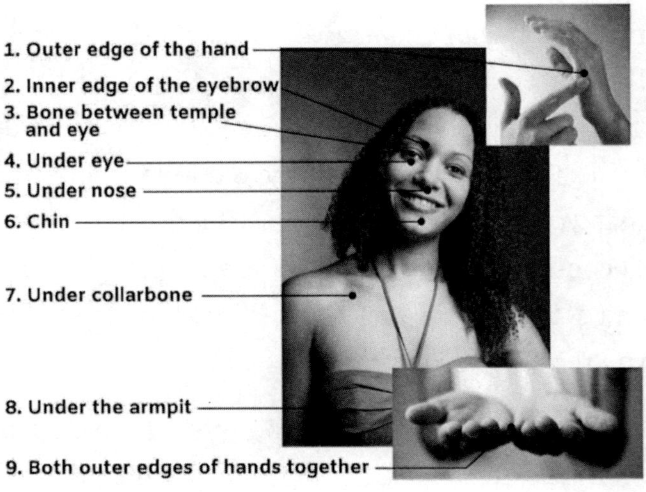

The idea is to tap each point very gently (you shouldn't feel any pain) in numerical order for as long as it takes. I'm giving a sequence here but it's optional. The important thing is to let the emotion out. You might spend ten seconds on one point and two minutes on another; it doesn't matter. It's absolutely necessary to say your statements out loud since your brain processes things differently through just your internal speech. Find a time and a space where you can have the peace and quiet you need. When I'm with my daughters, I do it in the shower or in the car on the way home from daycare. Get into a state of being in the present moment and start tapping on the first acupuncture point while naming what you're feeling. It can be: *I get so worked up when I can't do xyz. I have no willpower. I'm so sick of my f*ing neighbors who make noise until 2 am every single day.* In fact, anything that comes up and goes through your head while you're doing EFT is good. You can prepare sentences ahead if you want to but there's nothing better than living in the moment to name all your thoughts and emotions, even if it seems like nonsense. From time to time, insert the phrase *I accept who I am, just the way I am and forgive myself* into your speech and add *Access* phrases such as: *Everything in life comes to me with ease, joy and glory. How can it be better than that and what else is* *possible? In what energy, space, consciousness can I be for...* By doing this each day, you may not have to get rid of built up negative emotions anymore. We don't have to deal with unpleasant events every day, right? By clearing out everything you've accumulated, you'll likely feel better. Which would make sense because that's the whole point of EFT! What I do, after several months of releasing, is name out loud the goals I would like to achieve and all the thoughts that come up (which are mostly my limiting patterns and beliefs) and I break through them with EFT. Here are a few examples: *I can easily earn $100,000 a year by December 15th. I can easily lose 10 pounds by July 8th. I can easily meet the man of my dreams by June 30th.* It's important for me to add the word "easily" to make room for several ways of reaching my goals. For example, the fact that money can be earned in many ways. We shouldn't think that working harder is the only way that allows us to make more money.

Here's in short the steps I take to perform EFT[4]:

---

[4] You can do only one round of all the points by spending several seconds/minutes on each one or you can do several rounds of all the points. My EFT session varies between five and fifteen minutes each day.

1. Tap on point 1.

2. Name your goal out loud.

3. Name what's bothering you right now in your life as well as any thoughts that pop into your head in relation to your goal. For example: *I'll never earn that money. Who am I to be making so much money? I'll never be able to manage such an amount. Having such a goal makes me a person whose values are not in the right place.*

4. Say the phrase: *I accept myself this way and I forgive myself.*

5. Say the phrase: *All of life comes to me with ease, joy and glory,* h*ow does it get any better than this* and *what else is possible?*

6. Say the phrase: *What energy, space, consciousness can I be in for* X (rename your goal).

7. Repeat the same process for each of your goals.

8. Take the time to connect with the inner feeling that you get after going through the process.

9. Repeat daily.

CHAPTER 16
Relationships

Once you've connected to yourself, cleansed yourself from within, stopped hanging on to what doesn't belong to you, stopped judging yourself so harshly (sweet heavens, we can be crazy demanding of ourselves) and realized how awesome you are, something almost magical happens energetically. Magic starts working *for* us and brings us things we never could've imagined with our gremlin brains. Among these magical things, in addition to attracting different behaviours from people who are already part of your life (like, *completely* different), you start attracting people who really love you for who you are, who want you to be happy and who make you feel like a freakin' rockstar even when you're all messed up and doing nothing at all! Sick, right? It took me a while to get used to these kinds of relationships because the idea of incredible people showing love from all sides is difficult to grasp. Remember, being able to receive in abundance is not our strong suit! When we struggle to receive (I'm generalizing the notion to the majority of women because that's what I've observed in thousands of them over the past few years), it's often because we don't feel worthy. For instance, I once met someone who was completely amazed by my personality. I mean, completely blown away! And not when I was at my best, (when do you allow yourself to be completely yourself without compromise? Where you don't ask yourself questions? Where it's totally easy because we are just who we are, with all that that implies...) well ok, I'm an amazing girl so just *being* is my best. By the way, that's exactly the kind of thinking you should have about yourself, at the very least! So, I met this person and I was myself like never before. I talked non-stop, I was intense, stressed, a little bit awkward even. I was gesticulating so much that I knocked over my drink and made a big mess on the restaurant table. And the other person was just sitting there, looking at me and smiling. In her expression, I could tell that she was seeing in me a lot more than what I was presenting her at the time. She was looking at me as if she saw my soul. As if no matter what I was blabbering about, she connected with my essence, my naked self (seriously, it's kinda scary to write down). You know, that part of you that you almost never show anyone. Maybe not even your partner at this point for fear of being rejected, fear of being truly loved... It was so intense that I thought it was beyond what I'd asked for. Because yes, at one point in my life, I decided I wanted to up my game in regards to my relationships, which we should all do eventually. I wanted to be surrounded by inspiring and determined people who also have that urge to change the world!

So as I'm stepping out of this meeting, I tell myself that it's way more than I dared hope for. This person accepts me for who I am in such a way that it's almost frightening. But what the heck?! I mean, we undervalue ourselves so much that we're OK with being in relationships that drain a lot of our energy. I call this concept the +4/-22. You know everything that helps you a little in life but that also costs you a thousand times more in energy for being so cumbersome? For example, you have a job that gives you a certain stability but you're so unhappy in this job that it takes all of your spare change to get up in the morning and get motivated. You're counting the days until Friday comes. For me, it's a +4/-22. Or you ask a friend to come help out with the kids and she spends the whole day complaining about this, that and the other. That's another good example of +4/-22. In fact, the idea is that anything that helps you but ultimately weighs you down inside every single time represents a +4/-22 situation. Sometimes we mistakenly believe that it's helping us because we're afraid of being alone, afraid of change, afraid that the change will be worse than what we already have.

I now invite you, like right now, to take 5-10 minutes to examine all the spheres of your life (financial, social, professional, romantic, environmental, family, physical, mental, spiritual) to see, when you think about each one, whether or not it feels light. Whenever you have a feeling of heaviness, it's not light, right? Because if it was light, it would be at 100%. As soon as you feel a little twinge of discomfort within you, like something's not quite right, it's because you're lying to yourself. You don't completely respect yourself in this situation and something better awaits you. I guarantee you 100%

that when you choose yourself completely, it always pays off. It pays off by being beneficial for you. Whether romantically, professionally, financially, in your friendships or your health, there's always something better waiting for you on the other side of that decision. It's not necessarily an easy decision to make, I admit, but it's a decision that will make all the difference for what's to come, believe me.

Let's get back to that person who was looking at me in a way that made me feel like it was more than I could've ever imagined receiving. My friend told me, after I shared with her what happened, that it wasn't beyond what I could have expected, it's just that I wasn't used to it. *Wowwwwwww!* You know the kind of comment that, in a split second, completely changes your perception of something? I just wasn't used to being appreciated for who I really am yet, without the fear of disappointment, without the fear of being rejected, without the fear of being loved. Also being able to receive all this free approval just because I'm me. Period. I still get chills talking about it. From that moment on, I told myself that I would never again require anything less than this type of validation in all of my relationships and that's exactly what has happened in every sphere of my life. My partnerships, my team, my students, my clients, my friends. I began to surround myself with people who see me as the exceptional person I am. A sense of boastfulness comes over me as I'm writing these lines but that's exactly what happened. People can't get over how freakin' amazing I am and they keep telling me so.

Quick side note about myself; I didn't always have this many people around me who saw me this way. Again, it started from the way I saw myself and therefore, I attracted people who also saw what I was seeing. You feel me? If I find myself to be *meh,* well, my attitude and behaviours match with this vision of myself and I also make choices that are consistent with this meh vision. Of course, my circle of friends and family will be different if I perceive myself as freakin' awesome! I'm surrounded with such fulfilling relationships, so much so that when I meet a potential partner, I have an army of friends who want to make sure that he's truly worthy of the extraordinary person that I am. I say this very humbly as these are the facts. Be extremely careful of the value you place on yourself. As the saying goes, it's not the quantity that counts but the quality. Fulfilling relationships practically maintain themselves! You don't have to make any effort because you want to create magical moments with these people.

How are you feeling right now with the people around you? What's it like? Do you require the best of the best in your relationships? Are you getting all the love just for being you? In this very second, what's the number you assign to your self-value? Are you able to acknowledge that even when you judge yourself and are disappointed in yourself, you're still freakin' amazing?

Intimate Relationships

Now let's talk specifically about intimate relationships. Someone once told me about the existence of breath matching. Do you know what breath matching is? For me, it completely summed up how I see the relationship between two people. Sometimes you kiss someone and no matter what their oral hygiene is like, they brushed their teeth, they gargled with bleach, nothing can be done; it tastes disgusting... Well, did you know that it's all chemistry related? Also, it doesn't necessarily mean they have bad breath but rather that they're just not the right fit for you. So, this special person you're imagining yourself having a future with – if kissing them makes you feel nauseous, well, it's a sign that there's someone who's better fitting out there for you. OK, maybe nauseous is a bit much and I can hear judging all the way over here saying that there's more to a relationship than chemistry, sexual attraction and looks. That there are more important things than that. The fact remains that when you don't have chemistry, you make a conscious choice to stay in that relationship knowing it's your rational mind that has decided there was a match and not your intuition and your true vibe.

Do you believe in so-called signs? You know that you're the one who decides if the sign you're paying attention to makes sense or not and whether it's positive or negative, right? All this shows that a majority of us still have difficulty accepting ourselves and being ourselves while looking for someone to fulfill this wound, this need. Many people say that we must feel good about ourselves before entering into a relationship with someone else. Of course, if you're depressed or feel mediocre with low self-esteem and you're dating, you're likely to attract people who match what you're giving off.

When do you feel good enough about yourself to be in a relationship? I don't believe in that. You never stop evolving and becoming a better version of yourself. Others will say that you have to feel good when you're by yourself, that you have to be alone for x amount of time over the length of your last relationship, etc. Well, everyone has an interesting point of view on that. Most of them are not that happy in their own relationship. There's a minority of people I've met who really flourish within their intimate relationship. I find that really sad. Not that it's not OK for the others because it's just my interesting point of view on what relationships should be; but I still think that at the very least, it should allow both people to be themselves completely.

There's a space for this freedom including gratitude, kindness and without judgment for both people. Ideally, one should not NEED, but WANT to be with someone in their life because they make our adventure more enjoyable. The ones I've identified as unhappy in their relationships is only based on what I see could be different for them. I can confirm that most of the time, splitting up doesn't make people feel better but rather, getting to know themselves and therefore the other person better.

You may have made a nice list on paper of the criteria someone has to meet to be awesome. Girls don't do that, hugh? – making a list of qualities their prince charming has to have. Between us, let's be honest, we've all done it at some point in our lives. But if that person meets your criteria and you don't feel the attraction or, as they say, you don't feel like making out, well it's 'cause there's another person better suited for you! See ya! There's something better waiting for you. Not necessarily someone objectively better, just a better match for you.

Chemistry and Energetic Chemistry

Do you know the difference between chemistry and energetic chemistry? I'm sure you do. Many people describe attraction to another person as the "chemistry" between two people. Even scientists acknowledge its existence, despite being unable to explain it. It's not something that can be explained, it's a feeling. It comes down again to *being, not doing*. It's this attraction, this ease you have with another human being that makes us feel connected on a whole other level.

Someone asked me recently how I help my clients find perfect happiness in their relationships. Here's where I'm revealing all my secrets. First, I'll ask you to make a list including every micro detail you wish to find in the person of your dreams. No censoring. No judgment. Put in EVERYTHING that corresponds to who you are, to your level. I must admit that being a master chameleon, I often tended to choose men who were 75% of who I was and thought to myself: *Whatever, it's fine! I'll adapt to make the rest fit!* Does that sound familiar to you? I realized that I've used this strategy several times in my life. Out of fear of being alone, judging myself as superficial for letting minor details bug me. Until one day, I decided to honor myself, respect myself and be myself with my intensity, with my craziness and my excessive determination (according to others' interesting points of view). I embraced everything that makes me who I am. Really everything, including my worst flaws. And you know what? I met someone in love with it all. Who can ask for more? Can you imagine? The answer is yes! You can imagine it because it exists!

So people ask me how I help my clients find love; you know, the kind that makes you fall head over heels, that takes gravity away, that makes you realize life is worth living. You know? I sincerely believe that everyone deserves to be loved, that there's good in all of us and that even people who don't show it much have that lovable part deep inside them. Everyone can be loved for who they really are. Let's go back to the list that I suggested you make. Sometimes people will say, *Yeah OK, but I've already made that list.* And then I say: *Yes, on paper but did you also do it through your energy?* Let me explain. You may have made your grocery list of what your prince charming must possess to satisfy you; but if you don't sincerely believe that it exists, if you doubt that you deserve such a person, then your energy is far from creating this reality. In fact, it comes back to what I was telling you earlier; right now, you have the reality that you created for yourself. In order to create the reality of the perfect man for you, you must also attract him through your energy.

CHAPTER 17

Relationships Part Two - What Are You Gonna Do With Your Boyfriend?

Initiating a personal growth process and getting to know yourself truly will necessarily impact your love life. If getting cut off while driving affects your mood, if the weather affects your mood, it's inevitable that reading these pages and making all these realizations will change things in your relationship. It doesn't mean you'll split up but be mindful of the fact that things are gonna start moving! You may be with your spouse for any number of reasons: fulfilling some of each other's needs or conforming to some personal dynamics. For example, your inner child takes up a lot of space in your romantic relationship so you often need to be reassured (father/daughter dynamics). Not in a sexual way but rather in the sense that you need him to support and provide for you and in return, he needs to meet your needs to feel useful and rewarded. In this case, as soon as you start taking care of your inner child, it'll impact the dynamics of your relationship. Being in a relationship is like dancing. Since we are all constantly evolving, when one of the partners evolves in the relationship, the other will react by responding with their own movement. This doesn't mean that you'll be dancing to the same beat but there will definitely be some movement.

Complicity in a couple is when we manage to take enough responsibility to satisfy our own needs and we allow the other person to shine in the team (#loveteam). Too often, couples forget that they're a team, that they're *on the same team*. So remember at all times that you chose this person and recall the reasons why; because they were different from you, you liked them, they made you laugh, etc.

You need to adopt the role of the shine catalyzer. A role which, by its name, allows one to shine. How can you let the person who shares your life shine? You read that right! How can you allow your significant other to show off their best features? Imagine that your partner is Ovechkin, one of the greatest players in the National Hockey League. Ovechkin doesn't score his goals single-handedly. He needs his team in order to perform. How do you pass the puck at the right time, at the right spot so that your Ovechkin can score a goal?

What I observe most of the time is that we often assume the role of error inspector. We monitor the other person's actions in order to catch them at fault… so that we don't seem so bad ourselves in the end. That's far from true complicity, isn't it?

Developing complicity as a couple, or any complicity at all with another person, is being able to recognize what belongs to us and what belongs to the other person, making the difference by not having to take care of your own needs at all costs in order to be completely attentive to the other person. Complicity on that level is recognizing the changes of mood and emotions in our partner in the same way we can recognize a baby's cries. They raise an eyebrow and we know exactly what's going on inside their mind and how they feel.

For me, love starts from a feeling of excitement and butterflies in the stomach – or complicity, yes. It's also making the choice each day that tomorrow you'll still be in love with that person. Sharing your life with someone brings its share of uffffff. Getting to know who you really are, realizing that you have power over everything you go through, taking responsibility and deciding whether or not you're truly in love with your partner will make all the difference! I'm consciously and voluntarily choosing to invest myself and have a real relationship with this person, for who they are.

Of course, before we get to team accountability, we have to get through individual accountability. Commonly, spouses rely on each other to meet their needs which makes the relationship very burdensome, unsatisfying and more often than not, places the other person in an impossible mission. Our spouse is supposed to inspire us, bring us lightness and spontaneity. They're in no way responsible for our needs. When I share this view with my clients, I observe questioning and rethinking of their beliefs and their definition of a couple's relationship.

Now that you've decided to take the bull by the horns, what are you gonna do with your boyfriend who's reacting because you're shaking up the system? You tell yourself that his behaviour is pure nonsense and he doesn't understand why you're doing so much all of a sudden to try to be happy: *Come on, we were fine, weren't we?* You know what? In my experience, if one of the partners isn't happy, then the couple isn't happy either, right? Here you are, reading lots of things since the beginning of this book, you're making all kinds of realizations and you enthusiastically say to your boyfriend: *Hey, you know what, the reason why we're always fighting about this or that is because of this... Hey you don't know what, I was right about your mother being crazy, it's because of xyz. Hey, I regularly step into your world map, you too could make an effort and come into mine.* Oh, boy! You've now caught my wretched disease. You're speaking Chinese for a lot of people. Read the following carefully: *Just because you've made these realizations, doesn't necessarily mean that your partner needs to do the same in order for your couple to thrive.* Plus, between you and me, spouses don't generally like being coached by their girlfriend; it actually irritates them quite a bit.

#truestory

I have a client I've been coaching for several years who initially insisted that her boyfriend come in for a consultation. Sometimes, my clients fall into an I'm-already-the-one-who-does-everything-all-the-time-why-should-it-be-me-again-who-does-this-all-by-myself phase. My answer to her was: *You're the one who's aware of what's going on, so you're the one who has the best chance of getting the system moving quickly.* In my opinion, since she was a little bit fed up with feeling this way, she could embrace my interesting points of view and take ownership of the process. As I said earlier, before starting a process as a couple, it's often important to do a bit of work on your own to put yourself in a state of well-being first. You must be able to understand what you're going through and what you're feeling at a minimum before being able to be receptive and present to someone else. So my client agreed to come see me alone. From the very beginning of the process, she saw positive changes in her boyfriend. Surprised? Not really! Remember the famous system! If she reduces her stress, gets rid of her bitterness and has more joie de vivre, how can this not influence her boyfriend's attitude and behaviours? What's even more interesting is that one day, after about two years of coaching and without her boyfriend once seeing me in consultation, she left me a very inspiring message. She had just had a baby a few months earlier, her second child with her partner. She shared with me a discussion she had just had with him about his role as a father. How proud she was to have been attentive to what he was going through, to his needs, to how he wanted to live with the situation. All of this while sharing with him in turn how she felt, not simply accepting everything without saying a word. She shared her opinion and her tips to help him, without being judgmental and she even told me that they managed to have a real discussion where she shared everything she was going through and feeling while continuing to allow him to shine and to score. I was so moved to witness the quality of communication they had managed to develop over the years – and all without her boyfriend coming in for a single consultation! I was very happy for them. That's the way I work... I'm always very moved and very happy for my clients' happiness. It's 90% of my pay! The number of times I've written to my clients that I'm happy for them, I cannot count.

Doing this type of introspection in regards to our relationship can lead to a change in dynamics. As I told you earlier, there was very likely an initial dynamic that was present when you met each other. I gave the example of the inner child and the provider but there are several others, including the opposite, the inner child and the mother where the woman takes care of absolutely everything and the man voluntarily remains in a situation of never assuming responsibility. No matter what dynamic you and your partner are in right now, it's not that important. What matters is your awareness that if you change, this will affect the whole system, including your existing dynamic. A reaction from your spouse is to be expected and don't forget that when I say "if you change," I'm not necessarily talking about a huge transformation. If you've read up to this point, you've probably already made many realizations regarding your reality, which is enough to initiate change.

Another Anecdote

Brigitte, another one of my clients, decided that she was fed up with her lack of self-confidence and wanted more out of life – to stop feeling guilty about everything, to stop feeling that she wasn't good enough as a daughter, as a mother, as a spouse and even as a woman. I'm sure that just by reading this last sentence, you are able to feel all the heaviness of never being enough. Maybe that's what you're feeling right now and I sincerely wish for you to reconnect with the extraordinary person that you are.

My client came to see me about her lack of self-confidence but she never imagined that it would impact her relationship. In fact, her love life was going very well when she began consulting. Her boyfriend was a devoted and super-involved father, he heard her out, believed in her more than she did herself and encouraged her in all her projects. After working on herself for a year, after developing strong self-esteem and greater confidence, her boyfriend began to question her project choices and make comments that were a little unkind. He was reacting to the change. He obviously wanted his girlfriend to do well but the newfound confidence she was showing challenged his role in the initial dynamic of their relationship. That's why it's really important to trust the process and make room for your spouse's process as well. Her boyfriend needed reassurance that now that she almost didn't need him to encourage and help her believe in herself anymore, she wasn't going to leave him. This assumption is often made subconsciously but I nevertheless see it in the majority of my clients' spouses. It's exactly the same as when I was telling you about roles. If the wife no longer plays the role of "the one who lacks self-confidence", this has an impact on the role played by the spouse. By the time the dynamics of the relationship stabilize again, the spouse has gone through a period of confusion. If you're in this situation right now where you've updated your different roles and you've made several realizations, either by reading this book or through some other process, don't forget to take into account the influence you have on your system!

Finally, another thing to take into consideration during the process of working on yourself is timing. You decided to take this step, not your boyfriend. You have to do it for yourself first, without expectations. Without any expectations in regards to how it'll impact the system. And when I say without any expectations, I really mean zero, none whatsoever. We already know that *something* is going to change but there's no way of knowing *how*. And between the possibility that the change will bring your relationship to cloud nine and the possibility that the whole relationship will end, it might not be obvious. But there are a gazillion possibilities that you can't even imagine. I know that the void and the unknown can often be uncomfortable but leave room for wonder!

Another one of my clients was so excited about what she had accomplished for herself that all she wanted to do was share everything with her partner. You have to be careful though because as you know, most people don't like to be coached or told why they behave the way they do... I think we can relate, right? Being told by anyone, "Hey, I know why you have a drinking problem. It's because of that time when you were 8 and your mom told you yadi yadi yada..." The idea is, just because something makes sense to you, doesn't necessarily mean it's going to make sense to somebody else – and that's OK. The important thing is that you're feeling good because you're the one who's doing the introspection at the moment. We'll see how the system reacts in time...

However, sharing what you're going through obviously takes communication to a whole new level in the relationship. So, don't hesitate to include your partner but always be aware of their own rhythm, without expectations. They're in a relationship with you so this step you're taking will undoubtedly have an influence on their life. Everyone has their own rhythm of evolution. We cannot decide in advance the outcome of our relationships. The progress we've made in one year may take our spouse ten! Do you see the beautiful challenge that awaits you now?

CHAPTER 18

It's Not in the Doing, It's in the Being

Here we are! If there's one phrase that gets on my clients' nerves as much as, if not more than my famous "How is it helpful?" it's this one: "It's not in the doing, it's in the being that it all happens!" A client comes in to talk about her spouse. She tells me about what's going on, she shares her feelings and what she's tried to put in place that hasn't worked. After a few minutes of conversation, I established my meta goal: identify her problematic and make her experience the magic of NLP. What we call the meta goal in coaching is the goal of all goals. The individual comes in to address a certain issue, in this case a conflict with her spouse, but in reality, the source of the problem lies elsewhere. Hence the coach's job to establish the meta goal, the one that the client doesn't see but sits at the root of everything. If she reaches it, all her problems will be solved. If the person comes in for a conflict with their spouse, doesn't mean we'll be talking about it.

She tells me about what she's going through, I make her experience the magic of NLP and she feels completely liberated, in a state of total well-being. And then, at the end of the meeting, she asks me: *What do I do now?* And I answer: *Nothing! Your unconscious mind has already understood everything there is to understand. We've created a new neural connection. From now on, everything happens on the level of being and not doing.* I can tell you that it trips them up big time! We're so used to "doing" whatever it takes to get what we want, like the famous expression "You reap what you sow." In the case of my clients, to satisfy their need to *do* things, I sometimes give them little homework assignments even if I know that it's already resolved and I can guarantee you that'll do it! I may not have gotten into detail about that expression yet but when I say "that'll do it", I mean that come what may, once the new neural connection is created, it changes your perception of things and consequently, your attitude, your behaviours, your beliefs, etc. Success is guaranteed. Change has already happened. Hence the expression: "That'll do it!"

My clients sometimes have difficulty understanding this concept and accepting that they don't have to DO anything for their lives to change because we've been conditioned from a very young age to get praise for what we *do* and not for who we *are*. We're rewarded for making our bed, cleaning our room, getting good grades, behaving well, performing in sports – but rarely for making our aunts and uncles laugh by cracking jokes at the Christmas party. Another example is when a child often takes charge. We blame them for being bossy when in fact they show initiative and leadership.

Being and doing are directly related to self-esteem and self-confidence. You see, we have self-confidence when we believe in our skills, whether it's doing our job, cooking, taking care of our children or not questioning ourselves because we know we can do these things. Of course, the first time we take on a new position at work, we may be less confident but we have enough confidence in our other skills to take the plunge. Confidence is built by experience. By repeating the same action over and over again, we improve, become more skilled and gain confidence.

For example, if I ask you to go and teach a chemistry class tomorrow morning, you may doubt your skills if you don't know anything about the subject. However, if you enroll in chemistry classes and learn some teaching skills, your confidence will improve. After the first, second and 100th class, you'll obviously feel a lot less stressed and more confident!

Esteem is the value you give yourself which includes your qualities and flaws (I know you and I are perfect; I'm speaking about the others), who you are, your whole personality. I often repeat to my clients: *Being who you are is plenty enough to be loved.* Like the quote from rulestobehappy.com - rule 0139 that I find amazing: "Remember that being you is enough!" My god, that's so true! Being yourself is plenty! To have all the love you desire, to have all the happiness you desire, to have the life you desire. And believing in this, my friend, with a level of certainty like there's no tomorrow, will change the course of your history. Telling my clients that being who they are is plenty enough to be loved may seem like it's no big deal but each time, it causes a tsunami within them. They put so much effort into making sure they don't disappoint and always perform that when I make them realize that they can do nothing but just be who they are in order to be appreciated, they're in shock. It magically takes a huge weight off their shoulders. I know you're not like that, but you'd be surprised how many women do things for others before doing anything for themselves. Shocking!

Since most of us have been conditioned to be loved for our achievements and skills, sometimes we don't even realize the incredible personality traits we have. Are you funny? Are you smart? Are you generous? Are you messy? You know, all the beautiful qualities and flaws that define you. When my clients realize how extraordinary they are, it's funny, people just happen to make comments like, *You don't feel like coming to this activity anymore? Why not? You've changed a lot, I don't recognize you anymore...* And that's OK! People may no longer recognize you. You've changed, without them realizing it to some degree, and that can be unsettling for them. You know, it takes them out of their comfort zone... As they say, a relational clean-up is often initiated when we increase our self-worth. There are probably people who are in your life for what you can do and not for who you are.

Fortunately, now that you know how the system works, just because you start working on yourself doesn't mean you're going to end up alone. In changing our perception of ourselves, the people around us will also be influenced by this change since we are all interconnected. Consequently, we see different behaviours from these same people. And don't forget that there are infinite possibilities between staying the way we are and not creating changes for fear of being alone and changing to eventually end up alone. Human beings are full of surprises and capabilities! Don't underestimate their super power to adapt and evolve. Above all, trust the process.

It's in the being that it all happens, not in the doing. When you begin a personal growth process, the goal is to change your mindset. The very basis of it. That's what will change your perceptions, behaviours and attitudes towards different life situations. You can train your brain to change certain negative sentences by replacing them with positive ones. You can actually brainwash yourself by repeating these positive sentences until they become the new basis of your thought patterns. OR you can examine the usefulness of believing 100% that the statement is true and thus change all the other beliefs you have relating to it.

To help you better distinguish between being and doing, here are a few examples. If you're in the process of finding your dream job and you're exasperated over the past five places you've worked because they all had something you really couldn't tolerate: colleagues you didn't click with, uncompromising bosses, bullying. In the end though, if you're hired elsewhere for a similar position, you're operating on the *doing* and not the *being*. What are you doing that is smart enough to attract such working conditions? What's more, you think that all bosses are bastards who only take advantage of their employees and don't care about the quality of life and happiness of their employees. Now you know how this works. Do you honestly think that with beliefs like these, you'll get the job of your dreams?

If you're on the quest to find the man of your dreams, you don't stand a very good chance of finding him by sitting in your basement not talking to anyone. You need to take action. But if you focus on *he must be this age, he must do this type of work, etc.* and you don't even believe you deserve to have someone like that in your life, then I gotta tell ya, you're in deep shite. Making a list of the qualities you're looking for in the perfect man while you don't even think you deserve it! There's a little updating to be done here, don't you think?

Once you understand this concept and add to it a great deal of self-knowledge, the results become more than limitless. We take full control of our brain and none of our beliefs and self-sabotaging patterns can stop us. Take, for instance, a mother's courage when she sees that her child is in pain, is hurt, is going through a difficult time; she's ready to do anything to help him. Let's take it to the extreme. A mother has just had a car accident with her child inside the car. What could possibly prevent her from saving him? You know those stories about a woman opening a car door that was stuck or lifting up her car to rescue her child from underneath? It's clear that a massive dose of adrenaline along with other hormonal cocktails allowed her to accomplish this feat, but did she use outside help? Was she prepared or did she train for this kind of thing? No way. I'm telling you about all this to show you that there are many parts to each of us, some more laid back and some more courageous. Once we become aware of that, of what we're made of, that we are complex beings (and that's so cool!), we can consciously choose to activate this courageous part or not. I know, I'm repeating myself – but we really *can* do anything. I mean, do you realize how true and accessible this all is for each and every one of us?

So "It's not in the *doing*, it's in the *being*" requires a certain mindset clear up, starting with all those beliefs that prevent you from getting into action. If you think you're not capable of something, activate whatever you want to in your mindset so you can accomplish whatever you want! If you're not in the mood to do something, then get into it or make the decision to do something else! Everything you are makes you the exceptional person you are. It's now up to you to decide what you want to accomplish.

CHAPTER 19

Stand Up for Yourself, Woman!

This is the only chapter with a rather feminist orientation. At least so far... I can't promise anything. After all, I'm the writer of this book! My goal though is by no means to put a feminist bug in your ear, far from it! But facts are facts and when a woman stands up for herself, it has an infinite impact on who she is but also on the lives and futures of all the women around her. What is a woman who stands up for herself? It's not necessarily about standing up against men but rather about honoring who she is in all aspects of her life, respecting herself, demanding nothing less under any circumstances. I won't even get into the debate about pink razors that are sold to us at twice the price of green and black ones while in addition to that, we've been raised in a society that strongly urges women not to be hairy. I'd have enough material for a whole other book!

In the spring of 2019, I received a flyer in the mail from our local representative informing us that the government is going to inject millions of dollars in the next year in order to counter inequity between men and women, which is still very present in our western society. I'm currently reacting against Word which thinks I made a mistake because I wrote the female title for the word *representative* in French – *la députée*. It feels like my computer program (run by men) doesn't acknowledge women in power. Oh boy! We still have a long way to go, right? Do you get that when you write congresswoman or firewoman? I hope not. It might sound petty and I'm probably better off putting my energy elsewhere. But if you take a step back for a minute, you'll realize the extent at which we shrug things off, believing that we have no control over them or that it's not worth the trouble; but I digress...

So yeah, a tiny leaflet printed on a simple 8 ½ x 11 page, white, double-sided, in both French and

English. Honestly, at the time I didn't really know what to make of it. On the back, there's information about something else, not at all related to the previous message. It's obvious that for me, who's passionate about female ingenuity and conducts research on the subject, receiving this information without any specifics was shocking. At first, I told myself that I was in the right place to make a difference, that it was a sign that I still had plenty to bring to the world. Secondly, I couldn't help but feel outraged! In 2019, the government *still* has to inject millions of dollars to counter gender inequality – and we're only talking about job market wages here. Honestly, I didn't know what to think. In just 20 seconds, I'd received a smack in the face simply by picking up my mail. I'll tell you, my bills lost their number one spot in my mailbox that morning! I couldn't help but wonder why the government, the local MP, whoever it was that had come up with this strategy, would think of distributing information that ultimately wasn't saying anything. What kind of reaction did she hope to get from the public? A sense of satisfaction and security? Tell us that we're in good hands because the government cares about us? It was rather an insult to my intelligence. A feeble strategy to ensure women's votes in the next election. I'm not naive, I know how this works. Quietly, they place their pawns so they can weave the web that'll get them what they want. I'm not saying that the government is a huge puppet master, although...

I felt insulted and highly motivated at the same time. I kept the leaflet as a source of motivation for those days when I momentarily lose sight of my goal of changing the world and bringing female geniusness to benefit the maximum number of people. This simple leaflet is a reminder of where I'm headed.

Standing up for yourself is not about pointing the finger at a man or at anyone else you compare yourself to when feeling as though you don't have the same rights. Standing up for yourself is recognizing your true nature, honoring it and making magic, no matter what. Standing up for yourself is saying *no* to a friend who needs you to be there for her when you feel it's too much for you. Standing up for yourself is putting yourself first before anyone else. Standing up for yourself means making a commitment to yourself and giving yourself the best you have to offer. Standing up for yourself is never making compromises for who you are. Standing up for ourselves as women is embracing our wounds and turning them into strengths so we can break the generational cycle we come from and give our girls and all women an example to follow to change the world. I can't even count the number of clients I've supported in breaking generational cycles. It's not because where we come from is not OK that we have to stay in that mood. Tony Robbins puts it so well when he says that if we don't evolve as human beings, we die from within. Evolution is what brought us to where we are today. And by the way, there's always room for improvement.

Taking everything we've been given as far as our education, finding where we fit into all that, adding our personality and standing up for ourselves with conviction; that's what changes the world. It's not everyone's mission to change the world by fighting for what needs to be defended but did you know that being yourself has the same effect? Being yourself changes your world. Being able to be yourself in a world where everything seems to be common knowledge and everyone has an opinion about everything – changes *the* world. Take the time to be introspective, to stop riding on cruise control so that you can question yourself, yes; but above all, get to know yourself to the point where you can tell the difference between what's me, what belongs to me, what I want for my own life, without obsessively taking into account where I come from and what other people will think. I don't know about you, but writing this down is giving me a little “Ayayay”!

Now you might be thinking, “What do you mean, getting to know myself? I've been living with myself for x number of years, I think I already know who I am, I've seen all there is to see and I have nothing more to learn.” Good for you, really, if you think you've seen it all! I work with a personal coach, a business coach and a writing coach full time and I'm still learning about myself every day! All I'm saying is that when I talk about getting to know yourself, I'm not talking about whether you like banana flavored popsicles or not; I'm talking about getting to know ourselves on a whole other level. Knowing what our core values are. Knowing, without realizing it most of the time, what we stand for with our heart and soul. Why is it that sometimes, things that should be taken lightly in a relaxed Saturday night conversation, can turn us upside down to such an extent that it ruins our evening and we can't even get back to the vibe we were in 30 seconds before? When something strikes at our core values, our reaction can sometimes be irrational. These values define who we are and are tightly bound to our area of vulnerability. It's not surprising that we pounce like a lioness sensing her babies have just been attacked.

What's more, you need to know that these values were not necessarily with you when you were born. They make sense with who you are today and you hold them high and with pride because you've been on a particular path and have had wonderful adventures throughout your life (see how hard I'm working to change how you view your experiences?). There's also your environment and everything you've been exposed to, whether you've bought into it or not.

If I were to ask you right now to identify the three values that represent you and what you believe in, what would they be? I have a client, Danielle, who came to see me because she was having a great deal of difficulty feeling fulfilled in her role as a mother and feeling that she was a good mother. Not based on the criteria of her friends and relatives or society's definition of being a good mother, but what she would like to offer her children. When I asked about the values she stood for, she said: accomplishment, self-improvement and learning. She started crying and said she would never be a good mother, that she didn't even hold family as one of her main values... I simply pointed out to her that she didn't have the values that she idealized for her children but that she was her *own* priority. "What's best for your children: having a frustrated and unfulfilled mother or a mother who accomplishes herself and therefore has more patience, more understanding towards them and gives them an example of self-improvement?" Choosing yourself and respecting who you are is always the answer.

If you feel like this clashes with your values or if judgments or interesting points of view are rising, I encourage you to analyze what's going on there. Maybe you'll realize that it all stems from envy towards the someone who chooses herself when you wouldn't even dare.

Standing up for ourselves as women also means putting actions in place so that everything in our lives, no matter the sphere, is aligned with our values.

Do you have some cleaning up to do in terms of values? Just like your beliefs, your values need to be updated to reflect who you really are. That way, you won't go through life fighting against all odds because your values are not aligned with the person you've become. Just like my client Danielle, the idea is not to force you to buy into the value of family so that you become the mother you always wanted to be. The idea is to dig deep to find the essence of who you are in the core of your being, without judgment. Yes, I'm taking the time to focus on the non-judgmental aspect because no matter what you find there, it's definitely exceptional! Not exceptional in the sense that your head is in the sand, that everything you'll find is always awesome according to yourself, according to me or society. Exceptional in the sense that it's never good or bad. Here are some extreme examples to better illustrate my point. Whether you yell or have yelled at your kids before, whether you've cheated on your spouse, stolen, lied, betrayed, manipulated, basically anything that can make you feel ashamed of yourself – it doesn't change the incredible person you are because you're you. That's it! Whatever is making you constantly judge yourself about everything and anything that's in the past, just forget about it. It's useless and most likely false anyway, so stand up for yourself, girl! Stand up tall!

Dig out your inner pearl without judgment in order to put in place what's needed for you to feel good and happy. The goal is not to transform yourself and buy into a new set of values in order to be what you think you should be. Instead, it's about reinventing your role as a mother, according to you. For me, that's what it means to be a good mother to your children.

Standing up for yourself as a woman means recognizing the exceptional individual you are by simply being yourself and, in doing so, changing the world in your own way.

I am overwhelmed with emotion, strength, determination and an indescribable sense of faith as I'm writing this. Every woman in the world, regardless of their culture or religion, can connect with that diamond in the rough that sleeps inside her and can make herself believe that she deserves whatever she desires. Every woman has to implement her own reality, no matter what the goal is; fighting for women's and children's rights or giving them a good life, or being able to live a life without too much drama and feeling good, it's always OK. Everything is in everything.

#everythingisineverything

Standing up for ourselves as women is to say loud and clear that what we're going through is enough and that we believe in our power to make a difference in our own lives.

CHAPTER 20

Everything Is in Everything

I've been mentioning this since the very beginning and it's high time I explained the concept of "everything is in everything". This principle is so simple that it might be difficult to understand. It means that no matter what you think or do, in the end, you're part of a whole that is bigger than all of us, which causes everything to be intertwined. Regardless of whether you believe in God or in someone greater than us, in the energy, in the Universe or whatever – when you take a minute to think about it, we live on a huge floating ball called planet Earth. It just sits there, all by itself, in a dark galaxy surrounded by other planets which also, by the way, sit there all on their own. And I'm not even talking about the sun, the billions of gas balls called stars and the millions of planets that scientists have found in other galaxies which could potentially have the same characteristics as Earth. We have yet to find a way to get there. I like the idea of teleportation. Highly efficient, totally eco-friendly and completely independent of anyone else. I've been working on this in my free time.

It's obvious to me that there's something bigger than us. As much as we tell ourselves that we must take responsibility for everything that happens to us, that we are in charge and in control of our lives, the fact remains that I don't know of anyone yet who's been able to control the tides. Nuh-uh. The only thing you can do is surf the wave; you can't create the wave. Not yet anyway, but I'm working on that too. Also, when you become aware of this, you may realize that you've been working really hard, for quite some time now, on creating waves when all you had to do was get your board ready and surf the waves that are already there. What's the easiest thing to do? Creating your own wave or surfing the different waves that life sends you? Plus, you can choose! There's never just one wave and you can choose if and how you deal with each one. There's always an infinite possibility of waves and we have the power to make choices. You may think that there are many situations in your life right now that you have no choice but to face. Wrong. We always have a choice. The interesting thing is that the human brain has two reasons that motivate its choices and actions: either to avoid suffering or to generate pleasure. We always make the choices that are the least costly to us. What costs the least in your eyes: not having the opportunity to see your children every day for the rest of your life or staying in a relationship where you are slowly dying? This last option is very often addressed when I meet with clients.

Avoiding suffering is like if you start working out only when you realize you're really unhappy with what you see in the mirror or because your doctor says that your quality of life has deteriorated significantly due to your sedentary lifestyle. It's working out to make sure you fit into your wedding gown to avoid not feeling beautiful on your wedding day. Whereas to be driven by pleasure is to work out because you enjoy having better sleep quality and more energy even if you get less sleep. It's working out because you like to be able to follow your children around and hold them in your arms without running out of breath. It's working out to increase your energy to be able to accomplish even more of the things you love to do in your daily life. Do you see the difference?

My million-dollar question at this point is: what is, right now, out of all the things you're experiencing that aren't so WOWZAPALOOZA, the thing that would be most painful to get rid of? How is it pleasurable to keep it in your life? I know! Trick question huh? Right, you're telling me that there's no pain in reaching your goal and that there's no fun in staying where you are right now, but you're wrong. The good news is that if you take the time to think about it and you find the answers to these questions, becoming aware of this will automatically allow you to make different choices! Great, isn't it?

For example, you think there's no good reason for you to be miserable in your relationship, you've been together for several years now and you're just going through a rough patch. What if I were to ask you:

- In what way would getting better hurt?

Chances are, it's the fact that you see only one possible outcome: separation. You prefer to maintain the status quo even if it makes you unhappy. And now, if I were to ask you:

- What's the fun in staying?

You may very well tell me that it's nothing new, that this situation that's been going on for years is somehow comforting, that at least you know what to expect, etc. So you don't act, for all the reasons I've just listed, and in the end, the situation doesn't change.

Of course, you may decide to create your own wave. You can also consciously decide to continue surfing on pre-existing waves and transfer the energy you would have invested in creating a wave into something else. Let's be clear here, I have absolutely nothing against the idea of creating your own wave. We need women who create new waves. I just want you to make sure you're not self-sabotaging by believing that the *only* way you're going to be successful is if you do it all by yourself, that it's too hard and you're probably never going to make it as opposed to taking an opportunity that's already there, just waiting for you to grab it. If you decide to grab it while trying to avoid suffering, you're choosing the rough path. What are your reasons for not getting what you want? For example, say your goal is to make a lot of money with your business, but you believe that people will judge you and that you'll end up alone. Your will might be strong enough to make all the effort it takes to get there but you'll still end up sabotaging yourself. Who wants to be successful and alone?

When you're stuck in a toxic relationship, even though you know you're not happy, the thought of being alone or that you could do even worse are good enough reasons to stay in the relationship. The benefits of remaining in these situations are mostly related to the fact that it eases your fear of change. The notorious uncomfortable comfort zone! It may be uncomfortable but oh, so reassuring because we know it so well! This is only a tiny list of all the pleasures and pains you can experience. The important thing is that by taking the time to answer these two questions regarding your issues, you can feel major relief when you find the answer that makes sense. You'll know for sure that it's causing you to remain in the status quo.

I spoke with a client who mentioned that she didn't have enough energy to do all the things she wanted to do. That around 7:00 p.m. she would go up to her room and most of the time, she didn't come back down. *I have no other choice! My body needs a minimum amount of sleep to be able to function the next day.* Tips such as exercising, improving her diet, optimizing her time during the day so she could have some free time to do something other than work are all great advice. But the real question is: how is it useful to feel tired all the time? What came out was that having the excuse of being tired gave her a "good" reason to not do the things she didn't want to do; helping her spouse with yard work, having dinner at her in-laws', etc. In fact, always needing to rest and sleep allowed her to not live the life she had, in which she barely honored herself!

It's not that she was unhappy in her relationship or at work but she didn't share her needs and desires, thinking that it probably wasn't that important or that there was nothing she could do about it anyway. She realized that her parents had been telling her since she was a little girl: *Be careful, rest up, make sure you have enough energy so you don't get tired, be careful not to get burned out, etc.* Again, I want to remind you that the goal here is not to blame your parents.

The ultimate goal is simply reaching that awareness and once that's done, the unconscious mind records that new information. You'll never again be able to act like you didn't know. As a result, you will automatically change direction in your choice of actions.

As I said, everything is in everything! Did you know that all that surrounds us (the air we breathe, nature, human beings, objects, etc.) is actually nothing but emptiness? Allow me a brief biochemical aside. An atom is composed of 99.9999999999999999999% emptiness. Several atoms held together make up a molecule and we are made of these molecules. So basically, everything that exists is made of the same emptiness. So how can we regret a certain decision, a choice we made that has supposedly brought us nothing? Since everything is interrelated, everything has a causality.

A few years ago, I decided to sign up for a program for entrepreneurs to take my business to the next level. I wasn't doing well at all. I was unable to implement what the coaches were telling me since I barely had enough to eat and to provide for my daughters. We were a group of eleven entrepreneurs, motivated to push ourselves and come out of our comfort zones. One of the participants had a lot of health challenges, another one lived in her car. Can you imagine? At the time, I thought I should never have been in this program, that those who recruited me shouldn't have done so, knowing how seriously bad things were for me. Looking back now and understanding that everything is in everything, there was a reason I had to be in that particular group and not somewhere else. When I think about it, I realize that I met some exceptional people there who are still in my life today. Even if things were bad, even if I thought I hadn't learned anything (which is practically impossible), one of the outcomes of this event was rich human to human interaction. It always happens on the level of human interaction. Humans are social beings.

The relationship we have with the people we interact with on a daily or yearly basis, our children, our parents, our friends, is all that remains in the end. I've never heard anyone talk about how happy their life was as someone living alone in an empty house, without ever seeing anyone. Some people are less outgoing than others and the idea is not to desperately need others but still, people who never need to be around other people bear great wounds.

The other day, I went out for dinner at a restaurant with one of my friends. She's going through some big changes in her career. She's questioning herself a lot about what she wants to do and most of all, she doesn't want to give one more second of her time working somewhere she won't feel fulfilled and like part of something bigger than herself. It's OK if you're happy going back to the same routine every Monday and you're comfortable with that. But there are many humans among us who need to connect to something more; to have a life mission to invest in.

After a few minutes (more like a few hours), talking non-stop and making updates in our lives, my friend suddenly becomes emotional and confides that she finds this phase of confusion, incomprehension and uncertainty about where she's headed very hard to deal with. She also finds doing things differently from anything her family has ever done daunting. She's having trouble letting go of the idea of pursuing a career in her field of study. Having wasted all those years studying something, excelling, becoming an expert in the field in which she thought she would become accomplished, where she thought she'd found her path. Obviously, no matter which direction she decides to go in from now on, it'll be magical since everything is there, ahead, for her to create. Infinite possibilities. Her studies have at least allowed her to meet me and as it turns out, 18 years later, we're still friends. Hence the notion that "everything is in everything". If it wasn't for her studies, she wouldn't be exactly the person she is today. Maybe we would have met somewhere else, at another time. Our friendship certainly enables her to be this open and search for who she is in order to find out where she's going.

So when you can't put certain situations behind you and you can't let go of what's holding you back, take the time to look at where all these occurrences have led you or allowed you to go; or, most importantly, *who* they've led you to. When you think about it, everyone who's a part of your life is there as a result of a series of events that unfolded, without you noticing, until you met one another.

Which brings me now to talk about #thequeenofshit. When I'm in training with my students, I'm super demanding; my coaches have to be nothing less than amazing! They work non-stop. Seriously, I never let them out of my sight! They can all testify to that. They love it but after three or four consecutive days of learning and mostly experiencing NLP, they appreciate the three-week break between sessions. I must say that we joke around like nobody's business. To the point where, at the end of each training, we collect the hashtags that came out of it and we have mad laughs about them to this day!

One day, #thequeenofshit comes out. You can decide to be the queen of anything you want, yeah? When you start from the very beginning, you're at least the queen of shit! You might be called the queen of shit but since everything is in everything, I saw it more in terms of "get your shit together", aka straighten out your life, stop messin' around and get your mindset back on track. Which means that if you're in a situation where you have to get your shit together and you become the #thequeenofshit, doesn't that prove that you've regained control of your life and turned it into a mega WOWZAPALOOZA?

#everythingisineverything

CHAPTER 21

No matter What You Think of Yourself, That'll Do

I know. This title states the exact opposite of what I've been telling you all along. I don't care because it's too important to be dismissed. I always say that you need to acknowledge who you truly are, that you need to heal your wounds and to regain power over your own life. That hasn't changed. Once that's done, once you start creating your reality, what you think you need to do or be doesn't change a thing.

I've already mentioned that I process things in terms of "cause and effect". What you may not know is that I'm a cause and effect war machine! The queen! What does that mean exactly? It means that my brain links any information, as insignificant as it may be, with several other ideas that do not necessarily relate to each other, and BAM! I draw a conclusion. It's been such a lifesaver to realize that I must always validate my perceptions. When my cause and effect connect with my intuition, great things happen! It allows me to remember precisely what a client told me when we first met four years prior and make a connection with what she's currently sharing with me. Then BAM! Here comes the WOWZAPALOOZA!

Everyone has their own geniusness, as you know. I can remember tiny details that are often downright useless but that's the way my brain works. So, instead of judging it, I've learned to use it to my advantage. I have to admit that sometimes it's borderline insane but hey, when this super ability works in concert with my intuition, I can change the world. As you can imagine, my partner doesn't stand much of a chance! *I remember the exact date, babe, when you told me you were coming to my mother's birthday dinner. You were wearing those jeans, you were driving and we were headed to the spa on a Wednesday night for the two for one.* See what I mean? That's why when my coach made me realize that this is how I operate, I bought into the belief that no matter what I did or what I thought of myself, it would do. And that was incredibly liberating! As a result, I was honoring myself more than ever, in all spheres of my life. I had self-respect, I was listening to my intuition: my vibe, what tasted light. For sure, I was going to make it!

Because as you know or might be expecting – and I'm pretty sure many of you can relate to being able to generate cause and effect in a split second – when it mixes in with our personal lives and our emotions, that's when true creativity barges in.

Like the case of my client Judith, who's in the process of building rock-solid self-esteem and confidence. She wants to get rid of the impostor syndrome and let go of all her limiting beliefs about money. A major clean up! Honestly, she's making progress with lightning speed; true room-temperature butter! After a year of our monthly meetings, she tells me that she's still struggling financially. I tell her that it's only natural since she's not at all organized in her business. That's why the money's not coming in. I mean, what a limiting belief! It's as if there's always a reason to think that things won't work... Can you imagine the pressure associated with working on herself in order to operate in the *being* and freeing herself from everything that was holding her back? I'm not saying don't update your beliefs about money. For instance, thinking that becoming a millionaire makes you a bottom-feeder won't help you reach your money goals; but working on yourself to end up thinking that absolutely everything you do (or don't do) has an impact on your results is just nuts! It's as if going through this process for yourself, at the end of the day, has been for nothing. In addition to that, if in her everyday life she doesn't measure up, she doesn't do what she believes will allow her to bring in the money, she won't get any results at all. That's when I got her thinking: *What if you were wealthy, no matter what you did? If no matter the cause and effect you believe in so deeply, it couldn't change a thing about all the things you put in place to create your reality.* She then said that this concept finally relieved her from the huge weight of everything she had associated with her previous belief. And you know what? The day she bought into this new belief, because yes believing that no matter what she does, she will still get the results she's worked for since the universe never stops putting in place all it takes for everything to work out is *also* a belief, she made a new client and money started rolling in from everywhere! She even received a deposit to her account without having any idea where it came from!

If you work on yourself, get rid of your beliefs and have faith in yourself no matter what, the connections between who you are and what you do won't affect the outcome of what you want in life. That's why I'm telling you, that'll do! Beware of interconnections; they're actually just interesting points of view about ourselves. And acknowledge that creating your reality is much bigger than that, it's all about energy. Again, it's in the being, not in the doing.

Applying the Theory to Love

Let's say you meet a freakin' awesome guy. Let's say you can't get over how perfect he is for you, but then your gremlin gets into the mix: *Girl, you're way too intense! You seem desperate and clingy, there's no way someone can see you for who you really are and still appreciate you and think you're amazing. No way. That's too good to be true!*

I absolutely forbid my clients from saying that last sentence.

So we put ourselves in a mode of near paranoia, we analyze everything, we overanalyze our actions and behaviours, the other person's responses, the time it takes to answer our text messages and we tell ourselves: *Oh boy, I've gone mad! He's clearly gonna run away in fear, I'm way too intense!* What if everything you think about yourself didn't change anything about the situation? What if all these judgments had no power over the fact that you're an extraordinary person and you deserve nothing but to meet your perfect match? Because once you create your reality through energy (that may sound a little weird to you but since you read the chapter on relationships, maybe not), once you ask the universe for what you really want, there comes a period of confusion and discomfort. That happens when the universe puts what you've asked for into place. We often start to panic during this phase and we tend to go back on our decisions: *Well, I'm actually gonna go back to my ex, I'm not gonna change jobs after all, I'm not moving anymore, etc.* We chicken out, as they say, and go back to our uncomfortable comfort zones. I gotta tell you though, you have to bear with this unsettling phase as best you can and hang in there as long as you have to. In other words, I guarantee you that what awaits you on the other side is a hundred times, what am I saying, a billion times better than what you can imagine.

Once your conversation is clear and your requests to the universe have been made, remember that no matter what you do or how you are in the *being*, nothing can change what comes next. It's very liberating and on top of that, it prevents self-sabotage. It also helps you to hang in there when you're in the pre-change phase. So how does it make you feel if I tell you that no matter what you do or think, money will pour in? That no matter how you behave in the early stages of a relationship, it's not going to change anything. Sometimes people talk about certainty, faith, believing in themselves to make it work. But based on everything I've experienced these past few years, I can tell you that even if my client has doubts, that did it anyway! Isn't that wonderful? Sometimes (more like often), my job consists of telling my clients that it's OK if they don't believe it, that *I* believe it. And because of this certainty that I give off, they trust me and the magic of change happens in their lives. Just being yourself already makes all the difference. We are changing the world, as Dr. Dain Heer says. As human beings, we rock in our own way in this life, which pushes us, challenges us, transforms us! There are no challenges too big or too small. Just because what your neighbor is going through seems so much harder than what you're going through, doesn't mean you should dwell on that instead of making sure *you* are happy and content.

There. You got the basics. You know all there is to know, now you can close this book.

#not

CHAPTER 22

Your Why and SURcreating Yourself

Surely you've heard about finding your life mission; the great *Why*. There's this famous quote by Mark Twain, who said: “The two most important days in your life are the day you are born and the day you find out why.” In other words, find the reason why you were born, that notorious reason that makes you get up in the morning, that makes you strive for something bigger than yourself.

People can be motivated to achieve their goals in many different ways. Some people start making moves when they're up against the wall. For some, it's when they’ve figured out why they're doing what they're doing; others have that inner fire or that thirst for success no matter what. If you don't know the reason why you do things, why here and why now, your motivation will quickly dissipate. Do you know about the *eureka moment*? It is said to happen when we're in the shower or with both hands soaking in dishwater, after dinner for instance. As our brain activity slows down, it allows for momentum. Pieces of information that initially have no connection with one another and that we have stored in our brain suddenly combine. That creates a new idea which provides us with renewed motivation and tremendous excitement. But if the *why* is not present, the idea will shortly thereafter fall into oblivion.

Over the years, I've come to realize that I was born with this inner fire. This sense of being here on this planet to accomplish great things. When I set a goal for myself, nothing and no one can stop me from reaching it. Several people have asked me since I started my business when I would stop *trying*. When am I going to decide that I've tried hard enough. And if my goals haven't been met, I'd have to do something else. You know what? When people ask me that, it sounds like total nonsense to me. I've never thought about giving up or stopping. For me, it's clear that I'm gonna keep going until I reach my goal of NLP-alizing the world. There's no expiration date on my mission. Just recently, I was talking to someone I'd just met about my projects and what I do and she said: *Ok but what if it doesn't work out?* Once again, it blew my mind; my brain shut down, blackout. As far as I'm concerned, I'm going to be everything I need to be and that'll do! How about you now? What are your goals in life? What are your dreams? Are you committed to yourself so there are NO EXCUSES for you not to succeed? No matter your fears, no matter what you've experienced in the past, do you pull through?

One day, someone came up to me and said that it was only natural that she was having more trouble than me at sticking to her rituals, her routine that puts her in super power mode because I'd been working on myself for years. I make things happen. You can do the same f****** thing, by the way. I'm far from perfect and I have fears too but when I feel them taking over, when I'm really not sure of what I'm doing, like I might chicken out, that's precisely when I go for it, hard. I go precisely where my fears are. When I feel like I'm about to give up because I'm intimidated by the level of difficulty, I have no more reference points, I feel like I'm in limbo in terms of what I'm doing and I don't have the results I want yet, doubt is comfortably settling in like me in my lazy boy, that's when I close my eyes, take a couple of deep breaths and push through. I do whatever it takes!

During a conference by Isabelle Fontaine in 2017, I learned that courage can be developed and fostered. I bought into this belief. In the Maasai tribes, when they go in to snatch a lion's prey, they're armed only with a spear, their courage and a tiny straw skirt. Their demeanor is what causes the lion to let them take a piece of game and leave without reacting. In our modern Western society, we gotta admit that having to display such courage only happens on rare occasions. The hormones that secrete what's needed to build up this kind of courage are rarely triggered nowadays. We have to voluntarily create momentum inside us to crank up our courage level to the max, whether it's through music or rituals you perform each day to bring out the best in you.

It is not mandatory to have a mission that will change the world, far from it! I once met a man whose life mission, according to him, was to offer his children a gentler life than the one he had. Isn't that just as honorable? When we feel like we're doing things that are bigger than ourselves, we realize that we're not just doing it for ourselves anymore. We never do anything just for others, either. This father who's giving his children this incredible life is also offering himself some kind of redemption, a sense of inner peace from knowing that he's doing his very best so that his children don't want for anything. So they can have a good life in all the areas where he has the power to do something. Is he in some way doing this for himself? Yes. Is he also doing it for someone else and thereby participating in something great? Yes. He draws from his own experiences and scars to consciously offer something different to his children. And well, dear, that's what being brave enough to change the world is all about. By making a conscious decision to do things differently and especially by being a father with his own set of values, which are much more aligned with who he is, he influences the course of his children's lives, which then has an influence on the adults they'll become who will in turn, influence the world.

Everything we do has infinite repercussions that we'll never be able to trace... We'll never know the different influences these children would have had if he hadn't been the caring and loving father he's been. You can never know whose life will be changed because you decided to listen to yourself and finally embrace your life's mission. The repercussions, as I said, will be infinite. When you open yourself to the possibility that for the remainder of your days, you'll only listen to your intuition regardless of whether it leads to crazy ideas that are not encouraged by the majority of those around you; if it makes sense to you, it's the right thing to do. It definitely might not make sense to other people. It's not our rationality that drives us towards our mission. Usually, the source cannot be explained at all! All we can say is that we feel it in our gut! Don't let fear prevent you from living a life where your mission is so big and intense that you never need to be motivated by anything other than what's inside of you. You've already come this far, so as they say, give Caesar what belongs to Caesar. Give yourself credit for all you've done that makes you the extraordinary person you are and go for it!

As I said earlier, your mission doesn't have to include conquering the world. Whether your mission is to be a better father than the one you had or to decide that from this day on, you'll be happy as often as possible; all this is relevant! Remember the system. If you feel that you're doing something good, that it fills you with a sense of purpose and accomplishment, in what way do you think you're influencing everything that's connected to your system? If this influence makes everyone in your system feel better, it will also have a direct impact on *their* system. Do you see how quickly everything can have a domino effect? So don't underestimate the influence you can have on your own life, on the lives of others and on the world. Don't underestimate yourself, SURcreate yourself instead!

In life, we always have choices. Regardless of whether or not you think I'm right, it is what it is. I understand that right now, you might be going through a really tough time and you don't feel like thinking that if you're stuck in this situation, it's because of your choices. The fact remains that our reality is a result of the successive choices we've made. In order for our reality to be different, the choices we make have to be different. Like, completely different. Choices that take you so far out of your comfort zone that you probably feel sick just thinking about it. This sick feeling is a good indicator of change because most of the time, we think we're doing things differently but we're really not, as I explained earlier. We just use a different strategy to bring us to the same result, which keeps us in our uncomfortable comfort zone. That now brings me to the subject of SURcreating yourself.

There are different types of people in our environment. Nothing new so far. This is especially noticeable when you're working on yourself. It's not so much that there are people at a higher level than others, it's just that we don't all process in the same way or at the same speed. Some people will need only one coaching session in order to understand their dynamics while, you've guessed it, others require several sessions, wake up calls, therapies, etc. Right, there are also those people who never need help, who never need to seek counselling because everything is already going as well as could possibly be expected. They're just in a place where they think they're already OK and they really believe it. They may be right... We all go through a different process and the important thing is to be able to feel good each and every day.

The reason I'm telling you this is because it's all well and good that we have different paths and different paces. But what about you, in your environment? Where are most people situated? Are you surrounded by people who lift you up, who inspire you, who motivate you to surpass yourself, to excel? According to Stephanie Turcotte, neuro-potentialist and my personal coach, the concept of SURcreating yourself, which comes from Access Consciousness, consists of "always wanting to be better than who we were yesterday while always being proud of who we are today, no matter what we do or don't do; without ever judging yourself. You can't go wrong when you're SURcreating yourself because all you are doing is going above and beyond what you already know, above and beyond your immediate reality. That allows you to go towards even more possibilities and even more ideas. This means that no matter the area in which you want to SURcreate yourself or who you want to SURcreate, it's always done in a healthy way. It's about surpassing yourself without the burden and heaviness you usually get."

When you feel stalled, you can just look up and see what's already being done towards what you want to achieve and ask how you can SURcreate yourself based on that. For example, in one of my sessions with my coach, which I'll describe in more detail in the next chapter, I made the choice to SURcreate myself with Tony Robbins. I know, it sounds wrong when you say it like that and if your mind is slightly twisted, it can easily be misinterpreted. But anyways, the point is that it's important to have inspiring people in your immediate circle, or otherwise, who lift you up. Imagine the power of what you can create when you find and embrace your mission and then choose to SURcreate yourself on top of that in order to succeed! Oh wow; chills! The possibilities are positively endless... as always.

CHAPTER 23

Setting Things Up

One of the great gifts you develop when you start working on yourself is being able to bring visualization to another level. A level where we can set things up. What is setting things up? It's planting a seed in the universe but mostly in the subconscious mind. All of this is done with a specific goal in mind. When the person is ready, the seed will pop, creating a flash in their conscious mind and instantly transform their thinking.

Did you know that our brain doesn't know the difference between what it has seen in a book or a picture and in reality? Therefore, visualizing in great detail, i.e. seeing your success, tasting it once it's there, experiencing it (with images), detailing what you see and hear, etc. puts your brain in motion so you can reach your goal. Plus, as you create the image of your success, it's super important to be aware of any limiting beliefs that might cross your mind and possibly prevent you from succeeding. The majority of Olympic athletes do this. The difference between visualization and setting things up is that with the latter, deliberately or not, you take certain steps to make yourself aware of what you need to understand to transform your mindset. Like saying *yes* to a friend to participate in a race and then a few weeks later realizing that you kinda have to get in shape so you can do it. Like saying: *I'm not too chicken to write my own self-help book, just watch me!* and then realizing along the way that you're living your best life because of it. See the difference? You take action without obviously knowing the full extent of what it entails and what it leads to but you did *something*. You set things up! In contrast to visualization, where you foresee everything.

Anecdote

In the spring of 2019, I went to Mexico to give a conference during a business trip organized by the

RMA. I was part of a group of 24 businesswomen who had chosen to step out of their comfort zone, get inspired and shake things up with the different topics raised by the guest speakers. Since I'd gotten this contract several months prior, I had decided at the time to take my boyfriend along with me. The conferences only took three hours a day over five days, so in my mind, it was entirely possible to mix this trip/contract with some nice quality time as a couple. Winter settled in and even though things were still good with my boyfriend, during one of my meetings with my publisher Julie, I said: *You don't know it yet but you're the one who's coming with me on that trip down south!* She looked at me with a stunned expression and laughed nervously. *Good god, are you crazy?! I haven't had a vacation since my daughters were born!* Which meant over five years. It stayed that way until three weeks later, when my boyfriend told me that he had been unable to take time off work for the trip after all. Five weeks out from departure. I talked to the president of the RMA to see if she had any other people looking for a last-minute ticket, I made a post in the trip's Facebook group and lastly, I told Julie. She answered me directly: *Let me confirm with my boyfriend that everything is OK. I'm the one going with you on that trip!* Honestly, I was just blown away! I couldn't believe how easy it turned out to be! She confirmed her presence that very evening and that's when I realized that I'd "set things up". I knew Julie, I also knew her reality and I knew that she'd need to get organized in order to leave with barely a month's notice. When I pitched her that famous idea which came out of nowhere, I "set things up".

Setting things up is a bit like starting the universe's work. I show it the direction I want to take and it follows me in my own game.

In the last year, I also set things up for Tony Robbins. I don't know if you don't know who Tony Robbins is but to me, he's simply the greatest coach the world has ever seen. He's trained in NLP but has developed his own philosophy on human beings and to this day, has inspired and coached more than three million people. One morning during a session with my coach, I was telling her about what I was going through at that moment, which was that I hadn't found a mentor yet. Also, I couldn't find the training I needed to elevate myself, get out of my zone, and become a better version of who I am. She asked: *Who do you admire? Who do you want to SURcreate? Take inspiration from?* And then it hit me: I remembered that I'd been saying for a long time that I was going to become the female version of Tony Robbins!

With everything I do all day, I had completely forgotten about that! We talked about this on a Tuesday morning. On Wednesday, I saw an ad for Tony's Business Mastery course; a training program that I'd forgotten existed, that I'd been wanting to do and that I'd talked to my students about several months prior. I entered my contact information to receive more information. I got a phone call from one of Tony's assistants a few minutes later. I scheduled a call with one of his strategists on the following Saturday for an interview to see if I was in the right place with my business for this kind of training. A week after I gave my information, I was paying my deposit to book a ticket for the January Business Mastery in Palm Beach! Initially, I wanted information for the August training but I didn't know that I could still register for the January training. Also, I hadn't the slightest idea how I was going to pay for it; I didn't know that I could give a smaller deposit than what was advertised to secure my spot. You can be sure that since I had committed myself to this, there was no way I was going to lose my deposit. #noexcuses, remember?

I made different choices, I put myself in a different mindset to make it work. Without realizing it, simply by filling out the application form, I set things in motion. It's true that I was more likely to register by filling out the form but to be quite honest with you, with each step, my gremlin was telling me: *Stop what you're doing. You're wasting your time. You'll never be able to afford that kind of training program.* On the other hand, it tasted so light that my intuition was telling me to go for it!

People might think that when I "set things up" for my clients, it's like I'm manipulating them. Since I have the necessary hindsight, I can figure out what's really going on in my client's system. When I set things up, I do so by making a comment to which my client usually responds that it doesn't make any sense. That's perfect! *Huh?!*Yeah, I purposely say things that push the situation to the extreme and in all directions in order to broaden the person's perception. As we've already seen, people want to change but they don't want to do things differently. They're too attached to their comfort zone. By triggering my client with phrases, metaphors and ideas that they've never thought of before and that shake up their beliefs and values, I make sure to plant a little something different. Even if the person reacts negatively at first, the unconscious mind still picks up on everything. Sometimes this little something takes an hour to create change, sometimes a week or even several years. Eventually, however, clients tell me they can't believe how much what I used to tell them that triggered them at the time, now makes sense.

When you set things up, you're using your knowledge, leadership and kindness to help others. Just because you set things up doesn't necessarily mean that the person will take it; you can't force it on them. When you want to be a good leader for your family, for your children, for your colleagues, for your employees, you must use your strengths and the information you have that they don't in order to help them. Is that manipulation? Yes. Is it for their own good? Of course! By the way, if someone hasn't asked for your help, even if you spend all your time and energy trying to make a difference for them, it won't happen. They need to reach their point of leverage for change, which you'll learn about in the conclusion. I'll keep you on your toes until the end!

This is why, before trying to help anyone, it's essential that you go into their world map, without judgment and with curiosity and interest. These are the keys for improving all your relationships, my friend!

There's a difference between going into a person's world map and just *seeing* their world map. For example, one of your friends is going through an intense breakup. Going into her world map is being able to feel her pain and tell her that you understand how this must be hard for her. Even if deep down, you know he wasn't the right person for her. Only seeing her world map is seeing that she's going through a tough time but not understanding why since it's obvious that she wasn't with the right person. In both cases, you think it was not a good fit and you know that in the near future, she'll agree that she's better off without him. However, it's only in the first approach that she'll feel you're really there for her, that she won't feel stupid for reacting the way she does, even though she too knows very well that, rationally, it's better this way. It's only by truly being in her map without judgment that you can set things up in her unconscious mind. You can say, for example: *Can you imagine how good it'll feel for you not to have to adapt to him constantly?* If you're not within her map, I guarantee you that you haven't visited her reality, that she'll resist your comments and will probably tell you off, at least in her head! Alternatively, you can install something that will soon make her realize how much she wasn't herself in that relationship and she'll be able to feel relief. Do you see how huge the difference is? You have the power to create this positive influence in all spheres of your life. If you know yourself well enough, you'll even become a leader of change for yourself. For that, you're gonna have to start by freeing yourself from supreme judgment!

CHAPTER 24

The Supreme Judgement

I don't know if you've ever heard about how all human beings judge. Everyone judges everyone. This could be a way to get to know ourselves and define ourselves as unique individuals. I have formed an opinion on the subject through observation and I agree with this statement. Everyone always has an opinion on everything and nowadays, it seems to be mandatory to share it. What I've noticed most is that we judge ourselves even more harshly than we judge others. We can be so hard on ourselves, geez! Supremely hard; no room for error.

I associated this with the fact that our personal gremlin was multiplying. You know, like in the movie when he gets a drop of water and all of a sudden there are five more. Yeah, it multiplies five at a time!

Where exactly does our judgment of others and of ourselves come from? From our values, beliefs and strategies. For example, the other day I went to dinner with my students after a day of training. The restaurant was in a building that looked like a warehouse. So far, everything was OK with me but some of my students were wondering if there really could be a restaurant there. The waitress sat us down at a table in the middle of nowhere, near the kitchen and bathrooms. Honestly, I hadn't even noticed that the restaurant was almost empty. She could have sat us anywhere, but my focus wasn't there. It was only when one of my students mentioned it that I realized it myself. What makes a person focus on one thing instead of another? Depending on your values, you may or may not accept being placed at a table that you feel is not appropriate. Your beliefs will also influence your point of view. If you believe that in a restaurant you should be served a certain way, then there are inevitable criteria that have to be respected to determine whether or not it's OK.

I've also noticed that other people's points of view can make us judge ourselves. If you make a decision about your children and a friend makes a comment to suggest that maybe you shouldn't have done that, you then question yourself, maybe even to the point of thinking that you're not a good mother, that you're not giving them the best, etc. This comment is actually coming from your friend's gremlin. What you're hearing from your Gremlin is only interesting points of view. Nothing more.

If you only knew the number of interesting points of view about myself that I've had to undo. It's frightening! I was able to recognize the incredible person that I am *but* (the "but" that undoes everything) it was never enough. Let's say I set myself a goal of having five clients a week; once I had reached that goal, I was happy and proud of myself for like five minutes and right after I thought: *Yeah, but maybe I could have had ten clients this week.* And what happened after I reached my goal of ten clients? I would celebrate a good thirty seconds with feelings of gratitude for myself, realizing how amazing I am to be able to achieve my goals and then BAM! *If I can see ten clients, I can see fifteen.*

It's OK to have increasingly ambitious goals. I know that's how I roll. I always perform better under the pressure of a tight deadline. I digress a bit from my main subject but I want to share with you my ultimate tip on how to be as disciplined and achieve as many things in a single day as I do. I intentionally put myself in a mindset of being under the pressure of a tight deadline, even if I'm well ahead of schedule. Isn't that cool? While I'm writing these lines, instead of telling myself that I have x number of weeks left, that it wouldn't be so bad if I didn't write today, I get into a high level of performance energy. This way, I'm able to finish my projects before the deadlines. I wasn't always like that. Because I'm motivated by the "last minute rush", I've been in countless situations where I didn't think I was gonna make it and I'd be angry at myself for not starting earlier. The last few times this happened, I promised myself that I would never put myself under such stress again, that I deserved to finish ahead of schedule and be proud of myself. To have that feeling inside that everything will be OK without having to go to bed past midnight. You know what? It's true that being backed up against the wall is very "motivating", like you don't have a choice anymore; but feeling a sense of pride from finishing early is a million times more intoxicating!

I've also noticed that for most of my clients who are harnessing their geniusness, the strategy of waiting to be up against the wall in order to get them going is not uncommon. Being stuck in a dead end and being the one to come up with a genius solution is very rewarding! Plus, it's a well-known fact that such conditions allow the brain to function differently and push it to create new connections. So, they receive a lot of recognition in addition to saving the day, allowing them to take their business to a whole new level. And, let's be honest, they also enjoy being the saviors of a situation. How is it useful to wait until you're cornered before implementing strategies that could've been put in place a long time ago? How is it helpful when problems could've been prevented in addition to saving time, energy and money? Of course, not everything can be predicted but experience does come into play. If the situation is new, it's difficult to predict everything that may go wrong. Otherwise, what's the point? Perhaps it's to feel nurtured by that strong adrenaline rush and all the recognition that comes with it.

When we get to know ourselves, we become able to activate the right mindset to get the results we want. This means that if they want to, these clients can activate their geniusness at any time! Why do I specify "if they want to"? If they don't work out why they operate the way they do, they won't act any differently. For them, the benefits of operating this way are still too great versus their awareness of the situation. Imagine that they find ingenious solutions to every inconceivable problem in their daily lives. It would certainly create a dream reality worthy of who they are! No longer forced to put themselves in a difficult context in order to perform. That's proactive geniusness!

Yes, being demanding towards yourself can be OK. It can be alright as long as you do it with the intention of surpassing yourself or with the desire to become a better version of yourself, but without judgment. There may seem to be a fine line between thinking it's OK for us to do whatever because we're always the best version of ourselves versus never appreciating who we are because it's not the best version of ourselves. Think about that for a second. The best version of me is perfect right at this moment, as I'm writing these words. We're human beings and therefore, evolutionary beings. Technically, I'm now a better version of myself than I was yesterday. I have learned things, made connections that I'd never made before, etc. I'm a better version of myself than I was yesterday. I say "technically" because sometimes it doesn't seem that humans evolve much... Just kidding! Well, it depends who you're looking at! OK enough joking around, supreme judgment is serious.

So, if today I lie to one of my friends, I'm still the best version of myself. I did the best I could with who I am and my life situation while doing that. And then you have to ask yourself: *Who said that lying was not OK?* That's just an interesting point of view. *You're hurting your friend's feelings...* Well, maybe it's because that's what she had to experience. No, I mean seriously, there's no end in sight when you get into this kind of mental chat loop with yourself or with a friend who's just as crazy as you are!

I'm one of those people who are very hard on themselves. I'm extremely demanding of myself, my team and the people around me. They know this and they're allowed to bring me back to order as much as needed. Many people tell me that I'm not that bad.

Maybe not in real life, or they could just be lying to me, but I assure you that in my energy, I truly am! You might say that I'm too hard on myself, that it's useless, etc., but you have to know that there's a reason behind all this. I'm like this because I know what I'm made of and what I'm capable of. I know my own potential. And, like most of us, I underestimate it. In the sense that I'm even *more* awesome than I think! So how can I not be minimally demanding so that I don't waste all this potential? I realized early on in my coaching career that even though I see immense potential in my clients, the only people who can tap into that potential are my clients themselves. No matter whether I see it, talk to them about it, project it to them – if they haven't reached that point in their process or if they don't want to see it because they're not interested, they don't want things to change, what else can I do except set things up?

What I've had to learn over time, and believe me, it's still a work in progress, is to stop judging myself so harshly when I don't perform up to what I'm capable of. This applies to all spheres of my life, not only on a professional level. For example, as a coach, I judge myself when someone gets a reaction to a comment that I didn't see coming. I judge myself when I haven't formulated what I want to communicate to someone based on their world map. I judge myself when my mindset is not at its best. I judge myself for crying over a breakup when I know that, rationally, it wasn't for me. I judge myself for being extreme all the time. I judge myself for not always taking full advantage of the present by wanting to already be in the next moment. I judge myself for, most of the time, being only human. Do you ever have this kind of gremlin party in your head? Have you given the best version of yourself at any given time but not the performance of a lifetime as a human being?

On the other hand, that's the beauty of being human. All these judgments, all these interrogations, which ultimately make us question ourselves and see the infinite possibilities within us. Because deep down, what is "judging ourselves"? It's simply an interesting point of view. It's also knowing that we're capable of something greater, otherwise we wouldn't be judging ourselves. The goal here is to stop judging ourselves. Having an interesting point of view on what we should or shouldn't have done, on what we should or shouldn't have been is, let's face it, a fucking waste of time and energy! Trust me from experience, I've spent a lot of time and energy on this! And for what? How is it helpful to judge yourself? In my case, I'd say that it's still a way of not being in the here and now, living in the moment. While I dwell on everything that happened, I'm wasting my time. Can I learn from a situation and decide to do things differently? Yes! How do I do that? I hire a coach who tells me, more often than not: *Damn Marie! Are you done judging yourself?* It sounds absurd when you put it like that but it is what it is. I'm someone who's hard on myself, I take full responsibility for that and I really don't want to change that aspect of my personality. I'm even in love with the fact that I'm so demanding, productive and disciplined.

You know, my area of geniusness is powerful for others but much less so for myself. A coach is always their worst enemy when it comes to coaching. By knowing how I am and taking full responsibility for it, I've put in place a strategy to keep myself mentally sane and not spend most of my days judging myself. Judging myself when I am not living up to what I consider I should be living up to. This strategy is called Stéphanie Turcotte, my personal coach, Kim Grimard, my business coach, Julie Normandin, my writing coach and Peter Warne, my coach from the Tony Robbins team. Yes, I look like a freak for having so many coaches but how do you think I manage to perform so well and conquer the world? Certainly not by tormenting myself in my living room, not being able to do anything all this time!

This is MY strategy. The one that works for me. Everyone has their own unique traits, each with their own strategies! With everything we now know about human beings and all the infinite possibilities, it's impossible for you *not* to find what you need to get rid of your gremlins and out of your supreme judgment. And that, my friend, is simply amazing!

CHAPTER 25

Inner Child

Do you ever have irrational reactions? To such an extent that even you don't understand why that particular sentence your spouse just dropped makes you feel so upset? Experiencing great pain without knowing why? Wanting to do something like going on a romantic trip and coming back disappointed because it wasn't enough? It's never enough.

For example, my client Karine and her new spouse Sebastian are going to spend the day with her family. Sebastian is meeting his new in-laws for the first time. We can all agree that this kind of event can sometimes be a little bit stressful. We always hope that they enjoy our company and maybe even like us a little, you know! So, he goes to Karine's sister's house and everything is going well, the mother-in-law's outgoing, the brother-in-law's friendly. For a first meeting, everything seems to be running smoothly! But you know that can't be all there is to it and that something's about to happen because otherwise, there would be no point in telling you this story, right?

So, at one point, while everyone is sitting down, relaxing on the patio with a drink in hand, Karine says something to Sebastian. In a split second, out of nowhere, Sebastian becomes extremely defensive. Karine doesn't understand what's happening, she was just continuing the same line of conversation that was being discussed around the table. Sebastian is really upset; you can feel it very strongly and you can see that he feels attacked by Karine's comment. The day goes on as if nothing happened. Both know that something *did* happen but they'd rather wait until they're alone to talk about it. When that moment comes, Sebastian is unable to communicate. The only thing he manages to do is to bark completely gratuitous and hurtful remarks at Karine. At first glance, one might have the interesting point of view that he was wrong for acting this way with her.

However, many things happened for him in that split second and therein lies all the power of the inner child.

Obviously, this strong reaction shows that Karine hit a nerve. Unintentionally, of course. She thought she was making a harmless little joke, but we can agree that's clearly not what happened! What really happened was that Sebastian's inner boy felt like he did in the past – attacked, intimidated and belittled. But this time, in front of his new in-laws. He wanted more than anything to make a good impression. He thought his girlfriend was deliberately demeaning him. There was nothing rational going on in his mind at the time, to the point where he had forgotten that his girlfriend *also* wanted him to make a good impression. During their discussion, he had a childish reaction. His strategy was to rough up Karine; rejecting her before being rejected himself. Sebastian must've had some pretty intense experiences for him to react the way he did. We can also see that his self-esteem and self-confidence are not yet at a "heavy-duty" level. When we're in our adult state, we don't feel belittled or rejected. We're able to put things in perspective and realize that the other person simply has a different opinion from ours and that this does not take away from our value.

Do you ever feel scared as an adult? When you put things in place and find that what you're going through is weighing you down? What if I were to ask how your inner girl is doing? Your IG, for short, is the part of you that remains the child you were. This extraordinary child, who from birth was not under the influence of any belief or conditioned environment (which is more or less true if we consider that intra-uterine life influences our baggage, something I believe in, but we won't go into that now).

Who you are, as I said before, is the result of 30% your genes and 70% the environment in which you grew up, which activated one gene or another. So it's thanks to your IG that you're here and that you've learned what you've learned. I should warn you right now, if this is the first time you're hearing about your IG and you've never worked at this level, you may experience some very intense and highly emotional awakenings, like what you saw in Sebastian's case. Our IG still carries our wounds and everything we've been through as a child. If you don't take care of her, if you don't free these wounds, not only will you be dragging them along and allowing them to influence what you're creating in your reality, but your IG will become the manager of your system. What does an IG that manages a system look like? It looks exactly like what Sebastian experienced with his in-laws. He's afraid of being rejected so he may feel bullied with just one comment. He can't communicate like an adult. He's reactive and irrational.

It's like a client who came to see me because she's the head of her company but she can't answer her own e-mails because she's always worried about getting hate mail. Or like another client who has difficulty making decisions without consulting her parents and getting input from a whole bunch of people before taking action. Like a client who's afraid of judgment, afraid of failure, often overwhelmed by her emotions. When we're in our adult self, we're not afraid of failure. We know that if we do the right thing, we're going to succeed. We're not afraid of rejection. We're able to put things in perspective and say to ourselves that it's not so bad if our in-laws don't like us, assuming that's the case, because we're in a relationship with our spouse and not with all these other people. We don't give as much power to everything others may think of us because we know our value and don't question it all the time.

Here's what I suggest we do at this stage in the book: an exercise to take care of your inner child. Here's a little cautionary note though, this exercise can be quite intense but equally liberating. You may cry or you may not see anything, as this is a visualization exercise. Anything can happen really and it's all OK. What'll happen is what needs to happen; trust the process. If you find it too difficult, ask someone you trust to be there with you. It's always easier to go deeper when you don't have to read the notes while going through the process.

The Inner Child Scan

Here's one of my tools for taking care of your inner girl. It's an exercise that may seem very simple but one that will free you from many of your scars. I call it the inner child scan. You may have already worked on your inner child but it's important to check in from time to time and see if everything is still OK. Working on yourself is like peeling an onion. If you didn't work on something two years ago, chances are it won't be possible to do it that way today. You'll have to peel the more recent layers first. Also, even if your IG was doing great last time you checked, we can make sure it's still doing great. And if something very liberating happens, reading the book again with your *liberated* IG would be even more beneficial! You will most likely experience things differently the second time around.

Make yourself comfortable and take the time to settle in. Then close your eyes and imagine your inner girl in the room with you. Is she beside you? In front of you, behind you, on top of you, or inside you? Once you see her, observe how she's doing. Does she look happy? Does she seem cheerful? Is she sad? Is she scared? No matter where she is or what state she's in, don't stress; it's all OK. Once you're aware of her location and her condition, ask her what it would take to make her feel better? She can answer all kinds of things and all the answers are good, such as: feeling safe, having fun, feeling that you're OK, not being left out, etc. The goal of the exercise is to make your IG feel good and be by your side.

Do the exercise before you continue reading.

If she's in front of you, she's preventing you from moving forward. If she's too far away, she's not your ally and may feel rejected. If she's on you or inside you, she's managing your system. This means that you make your professional, romantic and budgeting decisions as your IG – in short, she influences everything you do and how you do it. Maybe many of the things you find difficult right now would not seem so hard if you did them as the adult you are rather than as your IG.

Your goal now is to ask her what it would take for her to agree to come out and stand beside you. Or what it would take for her to never be afraid again. Then, listen to her answer and respond back by telling her that now that you're here for her, no one will ever disrespect her again, that she's safe and above all, that she's amazing just the way she is, without doing anything or saying anything. Just being who she's always been.

Phew! My eyes are watering as I write, just at the thought of my IG. Feeling totally accepted, without any fear, just as we are in our own lives, no matter our age, is honoring and freeing ourselves forever from everything that's not us. We're often too scared to fully embrace who we are, fearing that people will judge us, dislike us, and reject us, so we adapt. In reality, what happens, after testing this myself several times in the last few years, is that as if magically, everything that used to get on your nerves or make you feel bad disappears or transforms itself.

I don't know if you know this but according to American author and speaker John Bradshaw, the two conditions that promote a child's transition into a happy adult are being loved for who they are and feeling a sense of security. That's it! It sounds simple when you say it like that but if you think about it well enough, how many of us feel loved for who we are as adults? Do we take enough ownership of ourselves to show the world who we really are so that people can love us accordingly? As you already know, it's not that our parents didn't love us adequately, it's just that our Catholic upbringing leaves no room for diversity and self-empowerment. We had to follow the rules or we would be severely punished. Children were a long way from being accepted for who they were; they had to fit the mould. When I look at where we are today, I'm so proud of how far we've come as human beings on that front.

I come across wounded inner children every day. Would you believe me if I told you that I carry around Playmobil figurines in my purse? When I see an adult who's carrying a wounded inner child, I give them one and tell them that it represents their inner child and that from now on, it's their duty to take good care of it. Yeah, it's a wonder I have any friends!

All the resentment you might be carrying inside you, all the bitterness you may be experiencing with regards to the hardest things you've had to go through in your life just go to show that you're giving too much power to these events. These experiences may have hurt you but they're now part of the past. As Richard Bandler puts it quite well, the good thing about the past is that it's over, so don't give power to what you don't have power over. Save your energy for all that you want to create in this life.

CHAPTER 26

Men Who are All That

I know that since the beginning of this book, I've been rather in a "girl power"vibe and that's exactly what I want. In all my years of practice though, I've also helped men transform themselves. There haven't been many since I have a predominantly female clientele, as you know, but I've had some men come through my doors. That's why I cannot overlook the extraordinary men I've been lucky enough to have met in my office. As I've already told you, in many ways, us women are very different from men and that's totally fine. Both are extraordinarily human. But a man who comes to an NLP coach specializing in working with super moms and says, *You help all these women, you can definitely do something for me!* OMG, that's so cool! I mean, that guy is so ready! And he's totally not going in there with cold feet, blaming the whole universe and feeling sorry for himself, no ma'am! He shows up proud of who he is, in spite of what he's here to work on, with a look that says: *Bring it on sister! I'm here now and I didn't come all the way down here for nothing!*

The Day I Realized that Guys in Coaching are *All That!*

A few years ago, I received a message from a colleague who had given my name as a reference to a friend of hers. He'd recently separated from the mother of his children and was in a new relationship, but he wasn't super happy. The reason for his appointment was that since splitting up with the mother of his two teenage daughters, he'd been having difficulty communicating with the girls. He came to see me three times. Each time, we were fearlessly real with one another. In other words, he was all-in! After only the first session, communication between him and his daughters had greatly improved. A few weeks after our series of meetings, I received a message from him. He thanked me, telling me that his life had never been better. He was in a whole new fulfilling relationship. In fact, he's still with that same woman. His daughter now lives with him and she also came to see me a few times. Despite the years that go by, I receive messages from him from time to time telling me that he will always be grateful for meeting me and for what I've done for him. You know, a guy who's willing to be accountable for his happiness.

Then there's Antoine, my client Caroline's spouse. Caroline had been seeing me through individual coaching for a few months when her spouse joined in. I first met Antoine in couples coaching and then individually. Antoine is a very rational man but he's also very connected to his emotions. A year went by before they came back to see me as a couple. After our first meeting, he'd taken the bull by the horns to the point where my client came back and told me he'd changed *too* much for her. She hadn't had time to adjust. Remember when I said to be careful what you ask for! Be prepared for the infinite possibilities! By bringing her husband in for counselling, she was convinced that separation was the obvious solution to their situation. When she saw her spouse get involved in the process, make different choices, become proactive in the face of changes in the system, she wasn't ready! When guys are all-in, it can move the hell out of a system!

Lastly, there's the spouse of another client. About eight months after they met, I was introduced to him in a normal setting. Sophie had a grocery list with several little things she was carrying around when we met. Things she didn't seek counselling for but once she had accumulated them, added to the fact that she'd seen my conference, she said to herself: *Why not?* Just for the record, it's not uncommon for my clients to come in with what I call a "grocery list". She starts to spurt out a whole bunch of unrelated facts but I can still see the common thread that runs through everything she wrote down. We often think that what we're experiencing is not important. We act like it's nothing and we build things up inside until one day, we give ourselves a shot at being completely happy and not just by letting go of the past, but by completely liberating yourself from the traces that were left by your past

Sophie and I then started a meeting that turned into a VIP and ended in a personalized monthly monitoring. She saw changes happen smoothly in all spheres of her life. Her relationship with her children improved beyond her expectations; the way she was managing her business, her health, everything changed! One day, I met her husband in a non-coaching setting. He thanked me for coming into his life. He explained that when I came into his wife's life a few months before, I had also entered his and since that very moment, I had saved his relationship and his family life. I was overwhelmed! I knew that things had been better for them lately but how could I have known that he was so grateful to me? In order for him to be able to share such thoughts and emotions with me, he was no doubt the kind of guy who wasn't afraid to question himself, who was confident enough to admit his mistakes and who wanted to become a better person for himself and his family. The full package, you know. At the same time, it's wrong to think that he *has* to be that guy. No, he *chooses* to be that guy. I find that particularly moving.

If you remember, we are not just one behaviour. Human beings are much more than that. So what was my client in that last example doing that was clever enough to get her spouse to behave in a way that made things worse between them? I'm not saying that everything relies on her shoulders, that she's 100%

responsible for their difficulties. But, when she became aware of the role she was playing, everything started to change. Because she had decided, several months earlier, that she wanted to do things differently from what she'd always known and what she'd been doing for years, because she was open, *she* was the person who would most likely generate change. Do you think her partner thought it would improve to the point that after 20 years of marriage, he was looking at his wife in a way he'd probably never looked at her before? No way.

Even my client, during the course of a session, realized that there were only two options in her world map. To remain in the status quo, which meant not changing anything and acting as if that's what love was all about, as if that's what married life was all about, or the second option: splitting up. How can we blame her? How can you think that after a 22-year relationship, after having children, experiencing illness, mortality, career changes, etc. and trying practically everything, that there would be any other options than to be satisfied with what you have or to separate? The status quo was not an option for her. That's why she had chosen separation. As you know, luckily a third option presented itself. An option that she couldn't even have imagined but which is a million times better than she dared hope for and which resulted in her husband thanking me for coming into their lives. Stories like that are part of my daily life. We are an infinite number of potentials that often only need to be seen from a different angle.

CONCLUSION

So here we are. We find ourselves at the end of this beautiful adventure. Now that you know me a little better, you must have guessed that I'm bawling my eyes out in my lazy boy as I finish writing this book... More than 70,000 words later, I still don't fully realize what I've just accomplished. Maybe for you it's no big deal but for me, it absolutely is. I just wrote a book! A fucking book that's been published in French and now available to the whole world thanks to this translation! So it's with great emotion and mixed feelings of fear and pride that I'm going to stir up your perceptions a little more.

Did you make a bunch of #deerintheheadlights faces? Are you now #roomtemperaturebutter, if you weren't already? Are you coming away with a "blank page in front of you, everything can be created and you can put anything you want on it" feeling? I still have something very important to share with you. Alexandre Nadeau, in his book *Miracles: Mode d'emploi*, says that if for us, in our world map, a miracle is winning the lottery, curing cancer or finding the man of our dreams, this means that we define miracles as something that can only happen once in a lifetime – and that is far from guaranteed. So what do you think that creates in your life? Do you suspect that this way of thinking will make you experience miracles on a daily basis or not? The idea here is not to redefine the meaning of the word *miracle* and make it become all the little daily things we do. The idea is to transform our world map with the recognition that miracles can happen every day and even several times a day! Can you imagine that scenario? Several miracles a day? So cool!

What do you think? Are you ready to live that kind of life where things just keep getting better hour after hour, minute after minute, each and every day? There's a plethora of answers you can give me. Since we've come to the conclusion, I'm betting on two options. Either you're saying to yourself, that's not what life is all about, it's too good to be true, #magicthinking or you're telling yourself that your life isn't that bad and that you're lucky to be alive, to be healthy, to have a husband who loves you, etc. Or you might be thinking something else entirely! I don't predict the thoughts of my million readers! I know I'm a bad chick but come on! Honestly, no matter what you tell yourself, remember what's most important: your feeling of well-being. While you might have everything one could hope for in life, if you carry a heaviness with you, it means you could feel better.

This book is only the beginning, I hope, of your adventure in learning about yourself. I sincerely hope that the insights you've gained will motivate you and make you want to dig even deeper so that you can live a free life that completely corresponds with who you are. I also hope that you've been able to internalize a few concepts and that you've been able to get rid of many of your beliefs that have kept you in the status quo zone. All that's left for you to do is make sure that you maintain yourself in a state of WOWZAPALOOZA by whatever means that work for you and make choices. If you take care of your inner state first, this will clearly have an impact and you won't make the same choices. If you are sad or angry, it will influence the choices you make. So, work on your well-being first and make the choices that will ensure you remain in that desired state of well-being.

Last little piece of advice: have more self-confidence than ever before. Be confident that all the actions you take with a feeling of lightness will never disappoint you, that's guaranteed. Make a pact with yourself, that from today on, you will lie to yourself as little as possible and if this is difficult to achieve, look inside yourself for the leverage that'll allow you to go from *"I should"* to *"I must"*. Tony Robbins says that everyone can change and all it takes is finding their leverage. The leverage that's going to make a person stop thinking, *I should improve my diet to be healthy* to *I must improve my diet to be healthy*. What's the difference when switching from one mode to the other? When you switch over to the "*I must*" approach, there's a conviction that takes hold of you, that says it's the decision you *have* to make versus not making a decision at all.

This *"I must"* can be motivated by several reasons but every human has within themselves this tool that allows them to stop believing that there are no solutions and that they will never be able to take action with NO EXCUSES. Find this leverage. Whether it's your children who motivate you, reaching your limit of suffering, your health deteriorating, your weariness of always being stressed financially. Whatever the reason is for pulling this lever, you stand up and say: *NO MORE. Never again will I live in poverty, never again, I'd rather die, let everyone die! I'm done! Never again will I feel trapped in my own life.* I know I sound extreme with my: *I'd rather die, let everyone die!* thing but that's exactly what leverage feels like. It's when you get to the end of your rope when it comes to your discomfort. When you're at your wit's end and you say: *NO MORE! It's over! I'm done with all of it!* You need to change tracks in your mindset and all your actions will align in a completely different way. Tell yourself one thing, if you're still in a shitty relationship, if you're still under financial distress, if you continue to gain weight, you're not fed up enough yet to reach your leverage zone and create change in your life. That's kinda harsh, isn't it?

#sorrynotsorry because right down to the last sentence, my mission will be to stir things up just enough to soften those beliefs that are yours and that shape your comfort zone, to offer you nothing less than all the infinite possibilities of life!

SECOND CONCLUSION

As you can see, I have become attached to you and I don't wanna let you go. Above all, I want you to have everything you need in order to free yourself from all that you're dragging along, to get rid of all that exasperates you in your life. And especially, I want you to realize what an extraordinary woman you are and that you have everything you need to reach your goals! Maybe you read my book in a day, maybe in a few weeks or maybe in a year. Either way, what I want you to see at this point are the changes that some of your realizations have brought about without you realizing it. What I would like you to do is complete your Wheel of Life again in the same way you did in chapter one. Redraw, re-divide, rename and re-evaluate. How is the outcome different? How has seeing everything you're going through with a different perception changed your life?

THIRD CONCLUSION

Just kidding, it's really over. Except for the final exercise on the next page. And don't forget to get your bonus on the website!!

Also, never forget: you're Amazing, Awesome and fucking *All That*!

EXERCISE AFTER READING

Let's play together one more time. Answer the following questions:

Who are you?

If you had a magic wand, what would you immediately change?

What are the challenges that prevent you from getting what you named in the previous question?

Special Thanks

I would like to take the time to thank myself because I'm a badass fucking boss girl who accomplishes everything she wants, who's an outstanding mother, who clears and leads the way for thousands of women and humans to choose themselves, to see the potential in themselves and to live a life even more incredible than they ever expected! And all this said very humbly! :P

Then, I would like to thank my daughters. They're obviously also amazing! As we say, like mother, like daughter! They are my best teachers for living in the moment, not taking life too seriously, laughing often and surely being more patient!

Thanks to my beautiful Elizabeth, through whom I found out what it meant to love a child unconditionally by choice. I just think you're amazing and being your stepmother has been one of the greatest adventures of my life.

Thank you also to my parents who, for one, have allowed me to be here. Secondly, who are the starting point of who I am and therefore, of everything I go through! Without this exact life I've lived, who knows if I would've gotten to write a book and even less THIS book! Thank you so much mom for giving me exactly everything I needed to be able to thrive the way I do and become the amazing person I love being today.

Thanks to my beloved little sister with whom I have a complicity that is out of the ordinary. With whom "Hello" in text is enough to understand each other and to know what the other is going through. I will never forget the home basketball league, the post-its in our college locker, our parties at the apartment, our girls' movie nights, all our St-Jean's, the crossings over into the new year, our gazillion hours of discussion, girls' nights having the time of our lives, our shared passion for *Pitch Perfect*, our cottages, our trips and so on. Your presence in my life has given me for a long time now the privilege of experiencing this unique kind of complicity. Your presence in my daughters' lives ensures that they'll always know what it's like to be loved so much. Thank you so much for choosing our family when you knew I was already there.

Thanks to my little brother, I'm your number one fan! I'm a real groupie of all that he is and what he accomplishes on a daily basis. I brag about the fact that he knows all about racing, four wheelers and sugar shacks. My brother is super awesome! And I'm even more in awe of the incredible father he's become.

I would also like to take the time to thank my publisher and friend Julie Normandin, who immediately, from first contact, made me feel like she was a bearer of great things and of magic so I immediately stuck to her. Thank you for believing in me and allowing me to have this amazing adventure! Thank you for seeing in me what I didn't yet see when we met. *Shit, Julie Normandin wants a coaching session with me! Shit, Julie Normandin wants to be part of my training!* You have no idea how much it has completely changed everything for me and how much having you in my life has made me aware of the chaos of the universe. And I'm ecstatic at the idea of playing the game of life and continue to be surprised by it, because I'm lucky enough to have you in mine.

And lastly, thank you to all my friends and coaches who believe in me more than I do myself. And of course, all my partners and clients who trust me every day to be the right person to help them transform their lives and allow me to accomplish my mission of NLP-alizing the world.

BIBLIOGRAPHY

- BANDLER, Richard, FITZPATRICK, Owen et ROBERTI, Alessio. « The Ultimate Introduction to NLP : How to Build a Successful Life » HarperCollins Publishers Limited Les éditions de l'homme, 2013, 160p.
- BEAULIEU, Danie. « L'art de semer : le pouvoir d'agir consciemment et autrement » Les éditions Académie Impact, 2010, 24p.
- CUDICIO, Catherine. « Comprendre la PNL » Éditions d'Organisation, Paris, 1986, 157p.
- DAVID, Isabelle. « Être au cœur de la PNL » Les éditions Québec-Livres, 1999, 176 p.
- DE ST-PAUL Josiane et TENENBAUM Sylvie. « L'esprit de la magie, la Programmation Neuro-Linguistique » InterEditions, 2005.
- ECKER, T. Harv. « Secrets of the Millionaire Mind » Harper Business publisher, 2005, 224 p.

- ESSER, Monique. « La PNL en perspective » Labor, 1994, 176 p.
- FONTAINE, Isabelle. « Le courage : comment l'activer? » Éditions Un monde différent, 2014.
- HEER, D. « Being you, changing the world » Lightning Source Inc Publisher, 2012, 338 p.
- NADEAU, Alexandre. « Miracles, mode d'emploi » Éditions Le dauphin blanc, 2017.
- READY, Romilla et BURTON, Kate. « Neuro-linguistic Programming For Dummies » For Dummies Publisher, 2015, 432 p.
- ROBBINS, Tony. « Unlimited Power: The New Science Of Personal Achievement » Free Press; Illustrated edition, 1997, 448 p.
- ROBBINS, Tony. « Unshakeable » Éditions Simon and Schuster, 2018.